**ANCHOR BOOKS**

A MOTHER'S UNCONDITIONAL LOVE

Edited by

Heather Killingray

First published in Great Britain in 1998 by
ANCHOR BOOKS
1-2 Wainman Road, Woodston,
Peterborough, PE2 7BU
Telephone (01733) 230761

HB ISBN 1 85930 675 6
SB ISBN 1 85930 670 5

FOREWORD

Anchor Books is a small press, established in 1992, with the aim of promoting readable poetry to as wide an audience as possible.

We hope to establish an outlet for writers of poetry who may have struggled to see their work in print.

The poems presented here have been selected from many entries. Editing proved to be a difficult task and as the Editor, the final selection was mine.

This anthology is a wonderful revelation of poetry full of emotion.

The poetry is delightful and is bound to bring a smile to any mum's face.

The poems vary in style and length but all portray to the reader the characteristics and splendour of mums and the wonderful jobs they do.

Both mother and child will enjoy this brilliant tribute to mothers.

I trust this selection will delight and please the authors and all those who enjoy reading poetry.

Heather Killingray
Editor

CONTENTS

My Dear Mother	Caroline Lester	1
Poem For Mother	Deborah Banks	2
Dear Mother	M Hanson	3
Mum!	Shereen Worden	4
My Mum On Mother's Day!	Kerrie Atkinson	5
My Darling Daughter!	Carol Fell	6
Mum	Vicki Griffiths	8
Who Am I?	Polly Lawton	10
My True Love	Laura Jayne McPherson	11
My Mum	Teresa Wild	12
I Remember	J H Bridgeman	13
Mum	Debra Elsom	14
Mother Love	Vera Fertash	15
Dearest Mother Of Mine	Joyce Taylor	16
Motherhood	Angela Isherwood	18
Priceless Treasure	Edith Cartwright	19
Where Would We Be - Without Our Mam	Ken Leigh	20
A Special Mother's Day	Jean P McGovern	21
A Recipe To Make A Mum	Harriet Matthews	22
To Mum	Nicola Susans	23
Every Day Is Mother's Day	Tony Connolly	24
Paul	Margaret Brown	25
Untitled	Elaine McKnight	26
A Mother's Love	Eve Armstrong	27
Holiday Mother	Jean Davies	28
The Plight Of A Single Mum!	D Rice	29
Passage Of Time	Margaret Rose	30
Motherhood	Christine Mogan	31
Flowering Love	Hannah Liversedge	32
My Dear Mum!	Jean Boughtwood	33
My Mother, My Hero	Louise Brennan	34
My Mother	Kathryn Lynda Lloyd	35
I Finally Found Time To Write	Madeline Dawson	36
People Would Say . . .	Jacqueline Fitzsimmons	37
Sorry And Thanks	Anita R Pickersgill	38

For My Mother	Lynn C Alexander	39
My Mum's Better Than Yours	Susan Young	40
A Daughter's Thoughts	Tracey Penn	42
Mum	Julie Ball	43
For Mother's Day And Every Day	Donna Kelly	44
Mother's Day	Anne Sackey	45
Baby Versus Body	Penny Brown	46
My Mum	Michele Simone Fudge	47
First Lady	R W Fleming	48
Mum's In Haste!	Sringkhala	50
Mother's Love	Susan Merrifield	51
A Mother's Words Of Wisdom	Betty Whitcher	52
Dedicated To My Mum In A Million	Kath Parsons	53
M o t h e r	Simon Peter Dennis	54
A Poem For Mother	Vanessa Mathison	55
A Mother's Love	Margaret Openshaw	56
Thoughts	B F Huggins	57
Letting Go	Jean Forrest	58
My One And Only	Tim Webster	59
A Tribute For Our Mothers	Christine Hartshorne	60
Her Parasitic Worm	P Hedgecock	61
Untitled	Ann Ardron	62
Grandma	Joanne Sarah Reeder	63
You Are . . .	Laura Epps	64
A Poem For Your Mother	Anna Bayless	65
Mother's Day	John Charlesworth	66
Apron Strings	G Noakes	67
My Weather Chart	Lindsay J Patching	68
Mothers Are Wonderful People	Edna Adams	69
For Mum	Helena Neale	70
Nursery Rhyme	Caroline Lee	71
Miriam	D Swallow	72
A Mother's Love	Sarah Carter	73
Mother	Beryl Sylvia Rusmanis	74
Mum's Birthday Bash	Sue Curtis	75
My Mum	Kathryn Moore	76

Make The Most Of It	Jack Sismey	77
Untitled	Thomas McCormick	78
Mother	G Harley	79
A Mother's Work	B W Crossman	80
My Loving Mother	Marlene Mullen	81
Untitled	Christina Hayes	82
Growing Up	L Starling	83
Pleasures!	Elizabeth Marriott	84
We Did Not Want	Marjorie Britton	85
Mummy	J M Grigor	86
To Mum . . . On My 40th Birthday	Wendy Hutton	87
My Mother	Val Taylor	88
Umbilical Cord	Carole Webster	89
To Mam On Mother's Day	Anne Craig	90
Untitled	Michelle Simpson	91
Mother And Child	R Costello	92
Thoughts Of You	Susan Moore	93
Essential Oils	Sarah Ledger	95
What's In A Mother?	Trudy A Williams	96
Untitled	Jan Beecher	97
My Mum	M H W Wildman	98
Mother Dearest	Sandra Pickering	99
Ode To Mum	Helen Rickard	100
Untitled	Irene Roberts	101
Mother's Day Message	Kulsum Shaikh	102
A Mother's Love	Karen Tyas	103
On Mother's Day	C C Warner	104
Mothers	Elizabeth Gorman	105
My Mum	Chris Hughes	106
Alzheimer's	Chris Gutteridge	107
Untitled	J M Dacosta	108
Bonjour Maman	Anne Polhill Walton	109
Mother's Day	Franciszek Bryszkiewski	110
A Tribute To Mothers	Vera Ewers	111
The Eyes Of Motherhood	May Perkins	112
Our Mum's Day	Jean Ray	113
More Than A Woman	Sue Elderton	114

Just For Mum	Elaine Marie Wilson	115
Mum	Carl Morris	116
My Mum	H Yates	117
Mother And Me	P Merrill	118
As Regards A Mother	M Lightbody	119
Mother's Memories	Lynda Marjoret Firth	120
Hands - Devotion	Aysha Rubeena Suraiyya	121
Untitled	Julie Mowatt	122
Be Still Child	J Christie	123
Mother's Day Wish	Ann Best	124
My Mum	Numero Uno	125
Summer	Margaret Poole	126
Almost Too Good To Be True	Vicky Wood	127
Three Cheers For Our Mum	Merilyn Gulley	128
Earth Mother	Louise Brown	129
Mother Mine	Lilian M Loftus	130
Mother	Tracy Bell	131
A Diamond Or A Pearl?	Jessie Morton	132
Three Cheers For Mum	Joy R Gunstone	133
Mother	Anne Palmer	134
Mother	Christine Sinclair	135
Lady Of The Flowers	Joy Cooke	136
My Mother's Love	Jean Carswell	137
Mothers	Iris Covell	138
Respite Care	Lesley James	139
Mum's The Word	Nichole Jackman	140
A Tribute To My Mother	Pat Jones	141
Devotion	Ann Beard	142
In Memory Of Her	S H Smith	143
A Tired Little Lady	Janine Dickinson	144
Mum's Seventy Today	Shirley Lidbetter	145
Mother	Evelyn A Evans	146
To The World's Best Mummy	Debra Wyatt	147
You're Always Near Us Mum	Lisa Wyatt	148
My Mother In Reflection	Chrissi	149
My Mother And I	Sheila Thompson	150
Thanks	Denise O'Donnell	151
A Mum Is Special	Linda Casey	152

Mother	Mary A Slater	153
Mother	David Sheasby	154
Mother	A Smith	155
Untitled	Maria Waters	156
Why Is It That Mothers Always Understand	Angela Bastiani	157
Three Cheers For Mum	Phyllis O'Connell	158
365 Days And A Quarter Plus	Donald Jay	160
Mother	Lydia McCubbin	161
Mother To Daughter, Is There A Spare Room In Your Heart?	Linda Coleman	162
Mum	Valvy Hope	163
To A New Mum	J Facchini	164
My Mother	L Coleman	165
Everlasting Love For My Mother	Alma Montgomery Frank	166
This Special Time Of Year	Rebecca Murby	168
Mothers	Ann Voaden	169
Our Mum	Pauline Uprichard	170
Mother's Day	John Christopher	171
Mothering Sunday	Jean Parkey	172

MY DEAR MOTHER

Oh Mother, Mother, Mother dear
Your comforting arms are always near.
When everyone is against you,
When nothing seems to go right
I long to hear your calming words of advice.

Oh Mother, Mother, Mother dear
Your comforting arms are always near.
I appreciate your understanding,
I love to see that knowing smile,
That reassures me all the while.

Oh Mother, Mother, Mother dear
Your comforting arms are always near.
It was a rare occasion for us to disagree,
I hope that I may be able to care for you,
As so many times you have been there for me.

Oh Mother, Mother, Mother dear
I hope your comforting arms - will always be near,
There are some thoughts I just cannot bear,
I could not stand to see your empty chair.
Oh Mother! Please will you always be there.

Caroline Lester

POEM FOR MOTHER

My mother taught me all she knew
But now she's like a child
It feels like I'm her mother now
for both a painful trial.

I'd like to wave a magic wand
And make it all come right
But that just isn't possible
No matter if I might.

There are some bits of Ma in there
If I look really hard
Perhaps it was her life to blame
Emotions badly scarred.

Remembering the way she was
Occasionally a glimmer
She fights a roaring tidal wave
A most determined swimmer.

And every time she seems to sink
We love her like no other
Yet try to pull her from the brink
You've only got one mother.

Deborah Banks

DEAR MOTHER

So good to me, you've been
Throughout my life,
So much in you I've seen,
Without trouble or strife.
What would I have done,
Without you there.
Always second to none,
Guiding me with care.
You show such great strengths
Through a broken heart.
But went through great lengths,
To give me a start.
My dearest mother and friend,
Keeper of my soul
For whatever I may intend,
Let me reverse the role.
Queen for the day, awaits you
Showing you a daughter's love
A family gathering, inviting a few
My special prayers from above.
Who knows what the future holds
Good times together, maybe forever.
In my dreams, hope is still alive
For this, is your day.

M Hanson

MUM!

This is a Mother's Day thought,
Ode to a lady that cannot be bought.
Flowers, chocolates or a diamond ring
Just don't mean anything.

OK she might moan
When things go wrong
When the house is a mess
And nothing's been done.

Sometimes she shouts
And loses her rag
Her hair stands on end
And she gets real mad.

But when you need a friend
And a listening ear
She's there with open arms
To welcome you near.

The voice of wisdom
That she is,
There isn't a trick
That she'll ever miss.

So who is this lady
So gentle and kind
That loves her family
And is always on my mind?

She's the person I grew up with
And she's helped me carry on,
This special lady
            Is my *mum!*

Shereen Worden

MY MUM ON MOTHER'S DAY!

My mum is very helpful
My mum is very kind
Whenever I've lost something
My mum would go and find.

My mum is very clever
My mum is very good
She washes up the dishes
And cooks our lovely food

My mum gives me hugs
She takes me to bed
She reads me a spooky story
And kisses me on my head

So at last it is Mother's Day
I will thank her for this
With chocolates and flowers
And cuddles and a kiss.

Kerrie Atkinson (11)

MY DARLING DAUGHTER!
(To mothers everywhere)

Do you have a teenage daughter,
Is she anything like mine?
Does she drive you to distraction,
Do you worry all the time?

From dawn 'til dusk does music
Bounce off her bedroom walls,
So she cannot hear the telephone
Nor door bell if someone calls?

Are clothes and shoes and handbags
Just strewn across her floor?
Do soggy towels soak the bed,
Are mugs jammed behind the door?

Does she leave her bedroom
Only to eat or use the phone,
And then does she chatter endlessly
To some other teenage crone?

Does she look right through you
When *you* want something done?
Do you become her closest friend
When she wants a lift at one?

Does she take you shopping;
Expect you to wait 'somewhere over there',
And then when you are summoned
Produce a wallet from thin air?

Do you love her dearly,
Would you defend her with your life;
Think she's the best there's ever been,
Worth all this toil and strife?

Take heart my friends, the teenage blues
Last only a year or two,
Then the mother and daughter relationship
Firms and sets like glue!

Carol Fell

Mum

The gates to heaven opened, the angels sang out loud,
A special lady was on her way that would make them
                                                    all so proud.
You're now with Nan and Grandad three stars that shine
                                                    so bright
And we know that you'll shine down on us every day
                                                    and every night.

This special message we all send with love,
And we know you're listening from up above
Our treasured memories we'll carry forever,
And again some day we'll all be together.

Thank you so much for being our mother
Thank you for our sisters and brother,
Thank you for being our best friend,
Thank you for fighting till the end.

We know you'll always be with us in everything we do,
Our lives, our future, our children we dedicate to you,
We know that you'll still guide us through good times and through bad,
And we'll feel your arms around us whenever we are sad.

You always taught us right from wrong,
With the strength you gave us we'll learn to be strong,
You showed us how to laugh, you showed us how to cry,
Always to be honest and never ever lie.

At this time it all seems so unfair,
When we still had so many things to share,
The feeling of loss we have today,
Will never ever go away.

We know in our hearts, you are now at rest,
Mum you were simply the best.
You are not to worry that we will suffer,
Thank you Mum you gave us each other.

Vicki Griffiths

WHO AM I?

Am I a mother,
or the other,
A *wife* maybe.

I cook and I clean,
you know what I mean,
A *housemaid* maybe.

I can't suffer ills,
I administer the pills,
A *nurse* maybe.

I know I've a mind,
I'm one of a kind,
I'm me!

Polly Lawton

MY TRUE LOVE

Age has greyed her youthful locks,
Her once-bright cheeks are weary,
All wrinkled is her furrowed brow,
Her golden eyes now bleary.

Her memory had faded since
She rocked me in my childhood
To hush away my every fear
As only mother mild could.

Alone, alone she takes her rest
And watches for each letter
Which brings a brightness to her days
Alone in age's fetter.

Her limbs no longer have the strength
To swing me in the garden,
But this and all her other faults
A loving child can pardon.

To me she is the only one
And I shall love no other,
No woman in the whole wide world
Is as lovely as my mother.

Laura Jayne McPherson

MY MUM

Oh my dearest dearest mum why did you have to go
To leave me with such a loss when I loved you so
You had so much to give this life with your caring ways
You were loved by so many, all of your living days
You had to give that little more but never any less
You brought to many a lot of love and happiness
If I live to be a hundred I could never emulate you
Or the kind deeds that you would take the time to do
The only reason I can think to why you had to go away
You had filled your good deed box up to that very day
It's at my darkest hour I know we are not apart
When I am feeling low I sense your spirit in my heart
It's then I realise the fact you live on in me is true
Because dearest Mum I am only an extension of you
I feel the strength you give me to bear any pain
To put my trust in God the suffering is not in vain
Each day I live I pause for a while wherever I may be
To thank God for I know my mum was only lent to me
But I pray dearest Mum I can join you there one day
So I shall try as you once did to earn my way
Along the path we all tread which leads back to God
And carry with grace my load that will test me
Because my most dearest kindest Mum I can now see
I have a head start on many people in this life
Due to the fact you left me with a wonderful legacy.

Teresa Wild

I REMEMBER

I am over eighty years of age myself
And remember my Mother's love and care
The seeds of good she sowed in my life
In many ways she made great sacrifice.

I was the youngest of a family of four
My Mother knew what it was to be poor
Small income, no family allowance in those days
But a great love and care was always there.

She taught me how to pray when I was young.
'Gentle Jesus, meek and mild, look upon a little child.
Suffer me to come to Thee, pity my simplicity
God bless Mammy and Daddy please, Amen.'

Such a prayer has taught me how to pray
Which is the important part of my life today
Each night my Mother sat me on her knee
Read stories from the Bible to me.

My Mother taught me manners and to respect
To use all day and wherever I went
When asking for anything I wanted I had to say 'Please'
And say 'Thank you' when I did receive.

All these were seeds of great love and care
It was the foundation stone which my life stands on today
I did not realise at the time how important they would be.
Prayer and my Bible mean such a lot to me.

The seeds that were sown on me by a Mother's love and care
Have grown in my life into large trees today
Prayer and my Bible are my mainstay
And I still think of my Mother each day.

J H Bridgeman

MUM

We went to the shop, we did your hair
To show you Mum, how much we did care.
Nothing you asked us, was too much trouble
Because dear Mum, you got a double.
Two of us, that's what you got.
Both Deb and Lynn to do the lot.
We did not mind, we loved you so
But now you're gone, we feel so low.
What shall we do now you have gone?
Our days are empty and far too long.

Debra Elsom

MOTHER LOVE

God knew when He made woman
She must be of sternest kind,
Well able to take suffering
Then erase it from her mind.
Love, to hold a new-born baby,
That she made, her very own,
Hers to cuddle and to nurture
With a love till now, unknown.
Fading fast the memory
Of pains she could just bear,
Tight in her arms the little boy
God sent for loving care.

Vera Fertash

DEAREST MOTHER OF MINE

Mother you think and study
Mother dream awhile
Mother you sit and wonder
At the beauty of life's smile.

Mother you are a precious gem
To me, your only child
Mother on days of stress
Your funny manner
Brings a smile.

Mother take your time
Don't rush at life
Cherish every day
Smile at everybody
You meet along life's way.

Mother sit and study
Mother dream awhile
Don't ever think to leave me
Miss your funny smile.

When I go to heaven
I know you will be there
Laughing with the angels
In your rocking chair.

As your arms enfold me
Hold me to your breast
My cup it runneth over
Together now we rest.

Joyce Taylor

MOTHERHOOD

Children, adults, everyone
Stop for a minute
And look at your mum.

Remember the good times
And all the fun.

She's brought you into the world
With one mighty fight
And wants you to put things right.

Stop for a minute
And give your mum a hug
Tell her she's loved.

Rearing you and caring
And taking all your tantrums
Give your mum a hug.
Her dedication, communication, control
And humour
Is shining out in splendour.

Meals on the table
Clean sheets on the bed.
How lucky we are
And what good times ahead.

What trouble we caused
And rows with dad.
Forget bad times, move on, move on.
The world is ours, and life lives on.

Angela Isherwood

PRICELESS TREASURE

There is no love like that of a Mother,
She is someone so special and fair;
It is love that is stronger than any other;
You know that she'll always care.

If ever you need her she'll be there at your side,
To help you along, come what may.
She will share in your laughter, from your tears she'll not hide,
You know that is always her way.

She's there in the sunshine, she's there in the rain;
In your absence she's saying a prayer
For you to return safe home once again,
To a Mother you know will be there.

So cherish this lady wherever you roam;
Give her your love in return
For all of the goodness and kindness she's shown,
It is the one thing for which she yearns.

Edith Cartwright

WHERE WOULD WE BE - WITHOUT OUR MAM

It's early in the morning
   And my dad's gone to work
I know my mam -
        Will stand no hassle.
With the time - a creeping
   To the school bell ringing
   And my shoe laces yet to be tied,
Where would we be -
        Without our mam?
She shouts - she scolds,
   With the flannel and soap
'Behind yer ears me lad' she rubs
   Comb yer hair - and blow yer nose
Let me look at you before you goes -
   To school - you'll be late again,
         I suppose.
Where would we be -
        Without our mam?
As I dash to school -
        In haste I do run
   To be met by my teacher
   It gives me no fun
I arrive just in time
   And much out of breath
My school cap askew
   And my face just like death

The rest is so easy -
   To which I abate
My mam just for once
   Indeed wrong - I'm not late!
But
Where would we be - without our mam?

Ken Leigh

A SPECIAL MOTHER'S DAY

Make Mother's Day, a special occasion
With surprises galore, and a celebration
And to make this day, so much worthwhile
To bring out her best, with a wonderful smile

Chocolates maybe her favourite, wrap them up with a bow,
Give her the gratitude, by thanking her so
For all the hard work, she has put in through the years
For being your mother, so precious and dear

Give her the joy, that she will never forget
A day to remember, so please do your best
Help her to relax, all the day long
Then she will do nothing, just to feel like singing a song,

When evening arises, make her to put up her feet
Entertain her once more, with such a nice treat
Even, play a musical instrument, she would like to hear
So the soft lilt will sound sweet harmony to her ear

Help Mother's Day to be happy, even with little gifts
So, she will know you care, and will give her that uplift,
And to give her happiness all the year through
As you gave her on Mother's Day, when your cares were so true

Jean P McGovern

A RECIPE TO MAKE A MUM

Take an armful of love and affection.
Place in a 30cm by 40cm tin.
Add a teaspoon of patience and mix
                                    gently.
Next place over 5 thousand kisses on
                            top and stir.
Add in a pound of kindness.
And an equal amount of love.
Put in a lorry full of support and mix
                                    firmly,
Add the Family Allowance Book.
Fold the mixture to let air in
            (So she can breathe)
Then leave for 20 minutes,
When finished, enjoy your mum!

Harriet Matthews (10)

To Mum

First I was born, you were my necessity,
When I was sick, you were my nurse,
Whilst needing attention, you gave me love,
At times of reprimand, you earned my respect.
Next came insecurity, you gave me confidence,
And lacking in discipline, so you set my boundaries,
When dwelling on problems, you showed me loopholes,
Walking blind through adversity, you were my guide.
Although now independent, I can still crumble,
Through hardship and pressure, and times when I stumble,
These frequent occasions, you're my only resort,
Because you never stop giving me your love and support.

Nicola Susans

EVERY DAY IS MOTHER'S DAY

Every day is Mother's day, as far as I'm concerned
One token celebration is the very least they've earned
All those years of worry, pain and anguish they've been through
Didn't have to happen, but they happened 'cause of you.

Always understanding, always there when you're in need
Recall the time you grazed your knee, and you began to bleed
Running to your Mother, thinking you were going to die
Then comforting her baby, she would help to stop you cry.

Remember when she cuddled you, when you were very small
The years have passed, you're older now, you've grown up to be tall
Never feel embarrassed, hug your Mother, make her smile
And those of you who've fallen out, one hug will reconcile.

In teenage years you tortured her, for trouble was your name
And though you hurt her many times, an adult you became
The strength of love your Mother showed was surely at its peak
That's why your Mother's special, and that's why she is unique.

Yes every day is Mother's day, as far as I'm concerned
You can't repay the love she gave, that's something to be learned
Cherish every moment and rejoice in all you've got
She won't be here forever and you'll miss her when she's not.

Tony Connolly

PAUL

You were my first-born
I loved you so much
But somewhere along the line
The apron strings got cut
But as the years have gone by
Deep in my heart, the love is still there
And I want you to know, I will always care.

I couldn't tell you this face to face,
You'd tell me to shut up and not be daft.
In the way that you do
But I'd give all I have Paul,
To hear you say

I love you.

Margaret Brown

UNTITLED

A sudden need to say hello
Draws me to Mum's today, and so
I look on from beside the door
While she sits unknowing on the floor
. . . Her favourite spot, so strange I say
As my thoughts turn back to yesterday.

I stand and smile as I recall
The times when as a child so small
She fussed and played and laughed and told
Me tales of elves and pots of gold,
Of fairies, witches, giants and kings
And oh so very many things
That still today ring in my ear
As I silently watch my mother dear.

My teenage years bring mixed emotion
As I recall the day Mum took a notion
To borrow my new French perfume.
This led her to a sticky doom.
She exited the bedroom fast
As flying hair to neck stuck fast.
For keeping up with the latest beauty tips
The bottle was filled with gloss for lips.

But later, when illness came my way
Her support has been my strength and stay.
Kindness, patience, understanding and care
Ever hide the frustrations I know must be there.
Her welcoming hugs, her open ears
Bring peace and solace amidst my fears.
A precious gift above all other
The priceless gem who is my mother.

Elaine McKnight

A MOTHER'S LOVE

A mother's love is stronger
Than the mightiest of men.
She'll be your friend and comforter
Time and time gain.

Her words may bring you pleasure,
She can bring you down to size,
But you know she's always there for you:
You're the apple of her eyes.

She knows your strengths and weaknesses,
Shared your deepest fears:
Watched you grow in confidence
As months rolled into years.

No one will ever love you more,
Or be so full of pride.
She'll praise each small achievement
And be there by your side.

Then as you grow to manhood
She'll step back a pace or two,
Knowing that it's your life,
The life she gave to you.

Not asking more than you can give,
A kind word is enough.
But mum can never be replaced,
So give her time and love.

Eve Armstrong

HOLIDAY MOTHER

A far cry from Kiss-Me-Quick on paper hats,
or giant dipper and the wheel of fortune -
although fortune brought us here.
And here and there a dipper of another sort,
alertly stalking sandy shallows
between the sparkling river and the shore.

And kisses of a different kind, unsolicited,
lingering without artifice on milky salty skin.
She is beady-eyed as any bird,
hoisting fledgling to one hip or shoulder high,
turning now, shielding brow against the sun
to pin-point trailing child.

No kaleidoscope of oscillating neon signs,
endlessly obliterating star-strewn sky,
to beckon us with tawdry choices.
When darkness falls, only moonlight silhouettes
the outline of a small café against the glimmering sea,
and owls swoop down from darker pines
encircling this gentle quiet place.

Piggy-backed and half asleep, we climb a winding path
and sniff the seaweed scent of sun-kissed arms
still clutching crabs in pails.
Late in night-lighted glow, I watch her bending low
to pull the quilted covers over sandy toes
and gently, barely breathing, lift the shells and
crumpled fishing nets from underneath their hearts.

Jean Davies

THE PLIGHT OF A SINGLE MUM!

You were not planned,
I can't deny,
a woman on her own.
How would I cope, two children
facing it all alone?
I carried on, determined,
Through both pregnancy and birth,
To prove to friends and family,
I could be Mother Earth.
Be mum and dad, to both of you,
Be there to hear your call.
Keep you warm, well-fed and always loved
and catch you when you fall.
Necessity had turned to love
Helpless baby no longer
Now a beautiful little girl
I sit back and I wonder why God has blessed my world
With a little girl, so precious, so pleasant,
and I touch your tiny hand.
Then I thank the stars, I saw it through
although you were not planned!

D Rice

PASSAGE OF TIME

It seems so very long ago since I sat beside your bed
To say goodnight.
Your hand I held, so fragile then
But in the past
Had worked as hard as any man.
Countless beings blessed that compassionate touch
That soothed so often, healed so much
In many ways, so many days.
Oft I looked in those eyes so blue
So full of fun.
With memory bright and sharp
For all your years.
A ready smile, a little quirk.
When telling tales of long ago
Oh! How I wish I had you now.

Margaret Rose

MOTHERHOOD

The clock is ticking over, my day is almost done,
The washing and the ironing have only just begun,
The Hoover sits there waiting, the mending's on the chair
The homework's done and dusted, brushed teeth, clean hands,
                                                    combed hair.
Just to see them sleeping peacefully, curled up warm and snug.
Makes every day worth living, I'm a mum and I'm loved!

Christine Morgan

FLOWERING LOVE

Roses
are red
but haven't
put me to
bed
like you.

Violets
are blue
but not
pretty like
you.

Daisies
are white
but hardly
ever right
like you.

There's
a yellow
buttercup
but it
hasn't
cheered
me up
like you.

Thank you very much!

Hannah Liversedge (8)

MY DEAR MUM!

When I was small and helpless, a tiny little scrap,
My Mother loved and cared for me, with never a mishap.
She washed and fed and changed me, just like all mothers do,
She hugged and loved and cuddled me, and cleared away the poo.

Now I'm adult and married too, my children tall and flown,
I can try to return the care, my Mum for me has shown.
For now she is not so able, her bones are getting old.
It's my turn now to shower her, and dress her for the cold.

I live next door, so nice and close, I'm constantly on call.
For hair wash, perm, or just a chat, I'm there to do it all.
Arthritis is a daily pain, and makes small jobs a task.
I'd do anything for my dear Mum, she only has to ask.

Jean Boughtwood

MY MOTHER, MY HERO

The precious gift of life you gave to me and revealed the
Wonderful person which I desire to be.
Cautiously you guide me along life's rocky road,
You assist me in carrying my heavy load.
You've watched me grow in both body and mind,
A friend as loyal as you I will never find.

Supporting me through every various phase,
You never fail to amaze.
You taught me the difference between right and wrong,
Showing me deep love all along.
Protecting me always from any harm,
Your influence keeps me calm.
You have taught me all I know,
Making me smile radiantly when I am low.

Your warm personality shines like the sun,
You have gave me forgiveness for all the wrong things
I have done.
You were formed in an original mould,
Your heart is made of pure gold.
My attitudes and emotions you completely understand,
When I need support you hold my tiny hand.
The love we share will never end,
You are my greatest friend.

Louise Brennan

MY MOTHER

My mother, my first love
Whose eyes held me close
And loved me completely.
Helpless I was then, cold or hungry
She was my warmth and fed me,
My mother, whose face I adored
Just to touch her was my total security.
As I grew nothing much changed
When troubles thickened, still, she clung to me
The strength of her counsel dissipated clouds of darkness
Until rainbows became visible.
My mother built me a nest but let me fly free.
Myself, now an adult, I understand much
And see by her eyes that she loves me still,
Completely and forever.
She rejoices in my successes,
Quiets my disappointments
And I love her so!
My patient, tender, brave devoted mother.

Kathryn Lynda Lloyd

I FINALLY FOUND TIME TO WRITE

Peace, perfect peace,
Now my toddler is in bed.
Time to sit back
And rest my weary head.

Thinking of the day
My exhaustion tells.
Madam got her own way.
She cast her little spell.

Tantrums and tears
And yet as sweet as pie.
Gorgeous little girl,
Even when you cry.

So clumsy and pathetic,
So headstrong and sure.
Demands for attention,
Then walks into the door.

Oh this peace, perfect peace
And a toy scattered room
Can I be bothered now?
It's just too late too soon.

I'm surrounded by the debris
There's pen art on the chairs,
Scattered, muddled,
A mix of puzzles lying on the stairs.

Yet beneath the frown marks and the lack of finesse,
I cannot deny,
That I feel I am blessed.

Madeline Dawson

PEOPLE WOULD SAY . . .

Remember the good times -
The times that we shared
And for a long time after -
I barely dared.
Because time and again
All that I could see
Was the child you became
And how you needed me.
But the most vivid picture
Filling my heart and my head
Is you lying still warm, but lifeless
In a hospital bed.
People would say . . .
But people don't know
How the aching for you
Continues to grow

Jacqueline Fitzsimmons

SORRY AND THANKS

I'm sorry for all the sleepless nights
The worry I caused and the teenage fights
I'm sorry for the tears I caused you to shed,
Yes even for those on the day I got wed!
I'm sorry for all the hurt and the pain
Yes, you're so right I'll do it again.

All the times that I said 'You don't understand'
All the times I fell down picked up by your hand
All the times that you hugged me and I never knew
Only this kind of love is the one that is true.

Now I've felt the sorrow, the joy and the pain
I've shed the tears, paced the floor just the same
Now I understand what a mother goes through
Oh, there's just one more thing Mum, 'thank you'

Anita R Pickersgill

FOR MY MOTHER

when mother held me in her arms
a baby newly born
I saw the love shine in her eyes
all pains of labour gone

through childhood ills, through cuts and scrapes
I'd sit upon her knee
knowing that she felt the pain
even more than me

when mother held me in her arms
a schoolgirl feeling scared
I'd take her hug to school with me
secure in love we shared

through bumpy roads of adolescence
with countless doubts and fears
through mood-swings, boyfriends, everything
she saw me through those years

when mother held me in her arms
a woman fully grown
she saw I had to spread my wings
I guess she'd always known

throughout the years I have explored
the world and all its charms
but I'll never be too old to fly
back to my mother's arms

Lynn C Alexander

MY MUM'S BETTER THAN YOURS

What does your mum do for you
Maybe my mum does it too?

> My mum shops and cooks the tea,
> All my favourite things for me.

What else does your mother do?
I think mine might do it too.

> My mum washes my best shirt.
> Looks after me when I've been hurt.

Your mum sounds just like mine,
She does those things all the time.
My mum's really lots of fun.

> I try to help get jobs done.
> Do you help around the home,
> Make your bed, answer the phone?

I tidy my toys away at night,
And always turn off the light.

> Can you think of jobs you do,
> Maybe I do the same as you?

I go to the shops for the bread.
Cuddle my brother when he's banged his head.

> I do those things all the time.
> Your mum really does sound like mine.

I empty bins and put dishes away,
I try to help a little each day,
We think our mums are the best,

Each one much better than the rest
They care for us in every way,
Look after us, join in our play.
But my mum's really the best you see,

No mine's the best 'cos she had me!

Susan Young

A DAUGHTER'S THOUGHTS

Right from when I was born
You meant everything to me,
You're the twinkle in my eye,
You're the sugar in my tea.

You gave me a home
I'd never swap you for any other,
I'll never let you go,
I love you so much, mother.

You gave me hugs and kisses
When I was sad and down,
When you are sat right near me
I feel so safe and sound.

The world is now a happy place,
Outside the skies are blue,
Guess what? It's 'cause you're here Mum,
Remember, I love you!

Tracey Penn

MUM

The pain of losing a mother has no description
You're torn in two and feel you have no direction
You wonder with each passing moment in time
Whether you'll survive the pain of losing a mother divine.

For 39 years you had been my mum
Caring each day with your powerful love
I grew up enveloped within your care
When I needed a shoulder you were always there.

Now you're gone, all you taught shall stay within
The light that shone brightly now flickers dim
An emptiness has devoured me and I miss you so much
Trapped in a state of suspension my memories I clutch.

Heaven invited you and you had to go
Goodbye mother, I love you so
I shall never forget each day we had together
These memories shall last me today and forever.

Each Mother's Day I'll reminisce your golden heart
And all the things and all the love I received right from the start
I'll close my eyes and there you'll stand with beauty and grace
This precious moment will keep me going and once again I'll feel safe.

Julie Ball

FOR MOTHER'S DAY AND EVERY DAY

Thank you, mother . . .
For every bright 'Good morning'
and every soft 'Sleep tight,'
For all the gentle lessons
that taught me wrong from right . . .
For all those reassuring hugs
and times you held my hand.
For helping me with problems - only
you could understand.
For knowing when I needed you
though not a word was said
For times you did without
because you put me first instead.
For all the ways you showed you cared,
when I was just a kid,
You may not think I noticed
but believe me, Mother . . . I did.

Donna Kelly

MOTHER'S DAY

Being a mother, oh! What a joy.
Whether your baby's a girl or a boy.
Looking to you to care and provide.
In return their love they don't hide.
Kisses and cuddles in the early years.
Make things better, and dry up their tears.
Years quickly pass, and their needs alter.
You hope they'll confide, and they will not falter.
Going out at night clubbing, you hoped they wouldn't go.
Wishing they didn't think, they are all in the know.
Disagreements I'm afraid there will be.
You only want the best, but they can't see.
Trust and faith comes with the passing of time.
Harmony will be restored, and all will be fine.
Happy days will outweigh the bad.
Children make you so proud, and ever so glad.
Each child unique in their special way.
Remembering their mum on Mother's Day.

Anne Sackey

BABY VERSUS BODY

I didn't think being a mum would come true
But my time has come and now I'm black and blue
What brain cells I had seem to have gone away
My tiny mind's not listening to what people say
Breasts have grown to a thirty-six double C
They feel like an implant that don't belong to me
Ankles are swollen and thighs are like jelly
They wobble about just like my large belly
Hair seems to have lost all its nice shine and bounce
And in weight I don't seem to have lost an ounce
My eyes look constantly tired and red
But there's no time to rest and go to bed
Is it all worth it, I hear myself say
Will I make it through until the next day
I then peep into the pretty new cot and see
A tiny little baby that belongs to me
My tears and frustrations then just away they melt
Then feelings of love come, the strongest I've ever felt
Despite my appearance it's the best thing I've done
This bundle of joy will bring such laughter and fun

Penny Brown

My Mum

On the day I was born, God's gift was to be,
A Guardian Angel to watch over me,
She would be there to nurse me through every fall,
To always be there for me whenever I'd call.
So throughout my life from beginning to end
I'd know I could always count on a friend,
How I remember the smells, as often she'd cook,
Tuck me into bed then read me a book.
She'd walk with me, talk with me, teach me to play.
Sing to me then share with me the joys of each day.
I'd then fall asleep when our day came to an end.
I knew I was loved so, by my cherished friend.
Now I am grown and she is still there to be,
The Guardian Angel the Lord sent to me.
He chose her a name which is second to none,
He blessed me then sent her and called her - my mum.
Each day that goes by I'm embraced by her love
My Guardian Angel, He sent from above.

My precious mum.

Michele Simone Fudge

FIRST LADY

I remember the times
When I fell off my bike
You always came quickly
To cuddle me tight.
Kiss it all better
But lift me back on,
Don't let this beat you
Little man, you're my son!

I remember the first day
In the village schoolyard
With tears held in check
Tummy knotted and hard.
Hold me forever
And then walk away
Be brave now my son,
You'll get through this day.

I remember your face
As I received my degree,
Fierce pride in your eyes
As you looked up at me.
My prize, your achievement.
You think I don't know
Of sacrifice made
That your son could go?

I remember the wedding
When I brought you my bride.
Did she meet your approval?
I could never decide.
Your pride and your joy
Passed on to another,
The victory of passion
O'er the love of a mother.

I remember the morning
When you met my first-born,
Wrapping him snugly
In the shawl I'd once worn.
In your face I saw beauty
As you looked at my son.
Age was defeated,
All the years were undone.

I remember I held you
As your spirit took flight.
In the dawn of the springtime
I kissed you goodnight.
It is evening now Mother
Love's duty is done,
Sleep well in the spirit
And soul of your son.

R W Fleming

MUM'S IN HASTE!

Metre Lady, stop a moment
just one second longer wait
it's a mamma hurrying shopping,
snatching grasping at the seconds
which betray her as they pass.

In her mind the seconds echo,
at her next stop a child is waiting
she must get to the school gate!
Tick - tick - ticking - tick
the seconds to the tapping of her toe
as she nervously taps the rhythm
of the anguish in her soul.
Ticket Lady, just one moment
do forgive her
let her go.

Sringkhala

MOTHER'S LOVE

There's no love to compare to a mother's -
A Mummy, Mama or a Mum
She's the one true best friend you can ever have
To seek solace, when life seems humdrum

No one more loyal, more trusting or reliable
You may try, but never will find
It's obvious to see why a mother
Is without doubt; simply one of a kind

With her own children grown, you can count on
Her support when raising your own
To help and advise and to guide you
The love of caring she always has shown

Stolen moments you always will treasure
Words of wisdom and knowledge, absorb
Cherish always the love of a mother
With pride, for one so adored

Susan Merrifield

A Mother's Words Of Wisdom

I have never written words that express the way
I feel,
But the love I have for my children is very,
very real.
I taught them how to love, to help others in
distress,
I taught them words of love, not hate or
bitterness.
I taught them to reach out to those souls so much
in need,
I taught them not to differentiate in colour, race
or creed.
Now that they have gone from me and have children
of their own,
I hope that from their early days the seeds of love
were sown.

Betty Whitcher

DEDICATED TO MY MUM IN A MILLION

Mother's Day comes just once a year.
So let's all have a jolly good cheer for her!
A chance to say thank you mum,
for all you have done,
all over the years!
We only ever have one mum,
so let's say a big thank you mum
for all you do 365 days a year!
We can always give flowers and chocolates,
but is there more we could do?
We give her a card and a big hug
and say have a lovely Mother's Day.
But we would like to show how much more
we care.
So I've put pen to paper instead,
to show how much we love you
all those 365 days a year!

Love from Kathleen Parsons   xxx

Kath Parsons

MOTHER

Mothers are everything yes that's what they are
They're there for you whenever you might need them
Yes we call them *Mum*
But they can be your best friend
You can talk to your Mother about anything
We can forget they teach us to talk before we can sing
All the things, that Mothers do
You might not be there for them,
But they're always there for you
To understand the meaning of a Mother's work is never done
I think you need to experience it or ask your *Mum*
They bring you into this world and give you all their love
Always watching over you, with the Lord above
I say a big thank you to all you *Mums*
All around the world forget your numbers or sums
They're the essence of life and make the world go round
We talk of heaven, well they're heaven bound
Because they never stop loving you
Just stop and think about it, I think you'll find it's true
No matter what, you might have done
They're always there for you, yes that's you *Mum*
They might not be there in body, but always in soul
You're always in their thoughts they play such an important role
Never-ending that's what they are
They take you on a journey, say they take you far
Yes you must learn to love and respect your *Mum*
Because they can tell you things before they come
They can teach you to win but they've already won
Yes and a personal tribute goes out to my Mother, my *Mum*

Simon Peter Dennis

A POEM FOR MOTHER

As a babe in her arms, she will rock you
and soothe away your fears.
As a child, when you fall, she will hold you
and brush away your tears.
She'll bathe you and clothe you and kiss you,
as she tucks you in bed every night.
As you become older, she'll guide you,
on a path that she hopes will be right
When you have a problem, she'll help you,
she'll be there to lend a hand.
When you need a shoulder to cry on,
she'll always understand.
When you leave home, she will miss you,
but she'll hide behind a smile.
When you get married, she'll be so proud
as you walk down the aisle.
You must cherish her, as she's cherished you,
for you'll never find another.
For unconditional love like this,
could only come from a mother.

Vanessa Mathison

A Mother's Love

Here comes the bride all dressed in white,
So beautiful in the bright sunlight,
But her life it will change and so it be,
When tiny feet patter in a nursery.

She glanced at her Mother who had started to cry,
Tears that thought Mother, the bride didn't know why,
They were pride that she once gave up so much,
To feel in her arms, her baby's touch.

Now at this moment seeing her married this way
To that once darling baby she wanted to say,
I pray for you to be a Mother like me,
And happy forever for your future to be,

There'll be dishes and cleaning, baby cries at night,
You'll need constant patience to bring a child up right,
And as they grow older and are out of your sight,
If you don't know what they are doing you'll get uptight.

Through all these years of laughter joy and fears,
That little baby did know the reason for her Mother's tears,
So gentle but firmly she took her hand,
And said, I love you dear Mother and understand.

Margaret Openshaw

THOUGHTS

'Mum' today my thoughts are of you
Your caring, and the good you do
Thoughts of love, and days gone by.
Joyous thoughts that make me cry
Your tender voice, and gentle ways
Remind me of my happy youthful days
Fields of green, skies of blue
Today they remind me of you
Hand in hand throughout the years
We've shared laughter and tears
Thoughts today came thick and fast
Let's hope today is not our last.

B F Huggins

LETTING GO

I'm smiling as I let you go,
My heart is breaking but you don't know,
I kiss your cheek and stroke your hair,
And watch you as you disappear.

But you're as happy as you can be,
It's your first day at school
You are leaving me.

Jean Forrest

MY ONE AND ONLY

You're my mother, and there will never
be another.

You opened your arms when I was young and
that's when my life began to be fun.

You understand when I suffer so much pain
and only being there, your love I gain.

So how could a mother be honest and true
so loving and tender, my dreams have come too.

Someone to hold and hug me tight and
telling me 'Son it will be alright.'

Just to know that you are there
that is why I will always care,

> I love you Mum.
>
> xxxxx

Tim Webster

A TRIBUTE FOR OUR MOTHERS

It's the time of the year,
Where children must be clear.
It's not the time to play dumb.
And say 'Oh sorry, I forgot'
The chocolates, books, music, the lot.

You must be generous
I know it's strenuous,
But think of how she will be
Of showing care, love and sincerity.

Yes, Mother's Day is unique,
And it takes a particular technique,
Which some still have to seek.

Christine Hartshorne

HER PARASITIC WORM

The parasitic worm, balder than innocence
Turns in the curlews of a swollen face.
And on that shivering moment
Tears up the file of prodigies
And burns its bearing thighs.

Like the girl who runs into the fawn and back, I ran down
Dreamed a boy's destiny,
Arms starting with warmth and not going on.
She gleamed in her eye and fell crystal still like waters,
Pillow and white like a flame

Like an old ghost waving the last goodbye
Calling on the end of a breeze
Sirens singing out for their Ulysses.
My love.
My mother - her last wave goodbye.

Feminine and heart
As white as smiles
A joy to be with
I watch you close,
Stand and shiver

Draw me
Cuddle me back as light,
Soft and cold as heart.
I warm my smile in your love
An eye for a long goodbye.

And now at the end of thy loving fuse
Thy courteous bones I tend,
Though the grave has no use
But thy loving soul to send
I wish my Heart . . .

P Hedgecock

UNTITLED

We often take for granted
Someone who's very kind
She guides us through our problems.
She almost reads our mind
We need her always to be there
To show how much we really care.

When we're young we need her.
She's always close at hand
If we feel unhappy
She seems to understand.
We share the good times with her
Hoping to give her pleasure.
With memories to fill her hours
Which she may always treasure.

Ann Ardron

GRANDMA

I have so many memories, from when I was small.
The picnics and the seaside trips, country walks and all.
Bilberry picking by the dam, Castleton ice-cream,
The resting-place of Little John and how we used to scream.
That's right scream, I see us now, and how fast we would run,
Chased by cows across the fields, now that's what I call fun.
Remember Rivelin Valley, and how we lost our way?
Treading through that marshy bog, as night drew in on day.
After hours of endless walking, we found your Viva car,
Got in, sat down and slowly smiled, then laughed 'til we were sore.
It seems like only yesterday, 'though many years ago,
But in those years, I became the person that you know.
There are no adults in this world, just children in disguise,
And it's the playfulness of youth that sparkles in your eyes.
Grandma, if it weren't for you, I would not be me.
Without your presence in my life, I don't know who I'd be.
So from one child to another, I just want you to know,
The love I hold inside for you will always bloom and grow.

Joanne Sarah Reeder

YOU ARE . . .
(Dedicated to my mum)

You are a lark soaring in the
sky brightening up my day.

You are a light, shining, leading the way
through the darkness.

You are a warm, cosy house with curtains
open and fires ablaze.

When you are angry, you are a storm cloud,
jagged in the sky.

You are a round, strong tree trunk standing
your ground while trees around you fall in
flame.

You are a soft feather carefully fluttering
and eventually falling on the ground.

You are my cuddly blanket at night ready to
cover me and keep me warm.

You are my favourite animal soft, furry
and lovely.

You are a glowing doorway with a mat on
the floor saying 'You are welcome here'.

Laura Epps

A POEM FOR YOUR MOTHER

The moment you're born, she's there for you,
And she stays there for you all your life through,
She's your anchor, your mentor, your leader, your guide,
And she will always find you wherever you hide,
She's your shoulder you cry on, your advisor, your friend,
And she will always be helpful, ready to give you a hand,
And you remember her touch, her sweet voice, her smell -
So I want her to tell,
Mum - you're the champion, you're the best, you keep me going,
And without you,
I would be totally lost and will not know what to do . . .

Anna Bayless

MOTHER'S DAY

It's Mother's Day tomorrow,
Let's buy Mum something nice.
'Yes,' said Josh 'let's do that,
How about a tin of rice?'

'Don't talk daft' said Laura
'that's no kind of a present,
She'll want something to look at,
A rose or something pleasant.'

'It's the thought that counts'
said Mummy as they set off for the store
'I've got your love and friendship,
and who could ask for more?'

This made Josh look thoughtful
As he went to bed that night
A present didn't matter
But the thought had to be right.

Next day a box of chocolates
From Laura was presented
The price had been reduced
Because the box was slightly dented!

'I didn't buy a pressie'
Josh said, coming through the door
'I thought I'd give you all my love
I can't afford much more.'

'I love you both' laughed Mummy
What more can I say
Thank you for the presents
And a lovely Mother's Day.

John Charlesworth

APRON STRINGS

Comfort and kind
Gives peace of mind.
A kiss in the night.
Takes away that fright.
A tasty meal,
With that loving feel.
She'll always be there,
For us, that's rare.
You hope and you pray,
She'll never go away.
You know you need her every day,
To get through life's tough task.
No need to ask.
It's much more fun,
Because you've got your mum.

G Noakes

MY WEATHER CHART

Amanda is so like the clouds,
She changes through the day.
One minute bright and cheery,
The next her mood is grey.
Thomas is more like the wind!
He rushes out and in.
He never does a thing he's told,
He acts on every whim.
Now Emily is like the sun,
She shines on everyone.
It doesn't matter what life brings
She takes it as it comes.
Edward is just like the rain;
He's always falling down!
He'll find his way into everything
You know when he's around.
Lastly there is Oliver,
A mix of sun and rain.
One minute he's full of laughter,
The next, full of disdain.
And so I have my weather chart,
The clouds, wind, sun and rain.
And tied with love around my heart
My rainbow will remain.

Lindsay J Patching

MOTHERS ARE WONDERFUL PEOPLE

Mothers are wonderful people
They're always there for you
They can be as strong as a steeple
And soft and gentle too.

They'll cuddle you, and hold you,
As well as anyone can
You'll love her for her tenderness
Your loving, endearing Mam.

Sometimes she will be cross with you
For things that bring you shame
But it doesn't matter how old you are
She loves you just the same.

So when she's feeling sad and blue
Return the love she gave
And you will find inside of you
The love that you both have.

Edna Adams

FOR MUM

For the person who created me
Who watched me whilst I've grown
Who's eased me through the teething years
Every tantrum I have thrown.

For the woman who has mothered me
When I was near to tears
Advised me when I came to her
With all my hopes and fears.

And for the person who has given me
The strength to be myself
To choose a life, become a wife
With family, love and health.

So thank you for my mother
And for the love you've shown
I have been truly privileged
To call my mum my own.

Helena Neale

NURSERY RHYME

'We'll attack it together' I told my spouse,
About the spare room in our house.
Our first baby was on its way,
And we needed a room for sleep and play.

'It won't take long,' I'd naively said,
(A can of worms soon reared their heads)
A light to be moved, plasterwork, filling,
Numerous jobs before *really* beginning.

My 'handy' Andy, quick and able,
Turned a chest of drawers into a changing table,
But a wardrobe, warped and needing attention,
Brought words from him I shouldn't mention.

The carpets and curtains were still quite new,
And happy were we with their shades of blue,
'But what if the baby *isn't* a fella?'
We decided to add lots of yellow.

Three walls in primrose, the smallest we papered,
Blue, with animals, was what we favoured,
But the gloss work turned out a *garish* yellow,
And was quickly redone in a colour more . . . ahh, mellow.

Wall hangings, mobiles, pictures complete it,
Cuddly toys in a hammock seated,
Watch patiently over the empty cot,
To the silent tick - my biological clock

'Not *too* blue, is it?' I asked with a sigh,
'No, *just right*,' he said, satisfied,
Our lives and that room were soon filled with joy,
At the gift of a new life . . . it *was* a boy.

Caroline Lee

MIRIAM

Tell me what I see is real
When I look at you.
Tell me what I see is true -
And not a veiled view of
Someone that I love so much
Who beholds a beauty that
I alone can see -
I am not wearing spectacles
Rose tinted or plain -
I just happen to be your mother.

D Swallow

A MOTHER'S LOVE

This mother's love for you, my son
Will never, ever come undone.
I've loved you through your baby years
When nappy rash and teething tears
Meant many an endless night awake and saw my patience wearing thin
But precious was that one first smile
That made those sleepless nights worthwhile.

This mother's love for you, my son
Will never, ever come undone.
I've loved you as a little child
When temper tantrums fierce and wild
Meant many a scolding word to make you understand some discipline
But precious things you'd do and say
Could melt my anger right away.

This mother's love for you, my son
Will never, ever come undone.
All through your teens I've loved you still
When moody sulks and stubborn will
Meant many a time my heart would ache as your own way you'd
                                            try to win.
But precious words my heart could please.
Those mumbled, shy apologies.

This mother's love for you my son
Will never, ever come undone
I'll love you too when full you've grown
When starting out all on your own
Means many a fall, but each mistake will shape the life you now begin.

Then precious hope I yearn to see
This mother's love return to me.

Sarah Carter

MOTHER

What is a mum?
You tell me because I am one,
You see I once had a special kind,
Someone who is so very hard to find.

She was so special in every way,
Perhaps very special, I may say
She was my heaven on earth
And that's not because she gave me birth.

She was my very best friend,
But never to comprehend
Anything that I insisted on
If she thought it best forgotten and gone.

I'll always miss and love her,
Though she has been gone for many a year,
She gave me birth,
A special angel who did once live on this earth.

Beryl Sylvia Rusmanis

MUM'S BIRTHDAY BASH

Mum's birthday bash was a big surprise, she'd
never been before, the greyhound track just a
short drive away so proud as she passed through the door.

A black limousine had arrived in the driveway
to take her along to the track, her eyes growing
wider as she saw all the splendour, not once
did she ever look back.

The excitement grew as the races got started,
the betting was high and intense, the old hare
was knackered as he ran round the race track
trying hard to avoid all the fence.

The high of the night was the race that Mum
sponsored, and the trophy she gave to the winner,
the cameras were flashing, the old hare still
knackered, just wanting his bed and his dinner.

A big family night was enjoyed by us all, it's
so nice when our family is together,
make the most of lour time what we have on this
earth, as good things won't last for ever.

Sue Curtis

MY MUM

Mum you are fun
You play with me
You take me out
You make me tea
Mum I'm trying to tell you I love you.

Mum you wash my clothes
You buy me things
If they break you sew them together
Mum I'm trying to tell you I love you.

Kathryn Moore (6)

MAKE THE MOST OF IT

The day is coming, the day is near
The day for your mother
That's so full of cheer
You give flowers and other little things
For you to express the joy that she brings

They have nursed you and fed you
Through the length of your life
Many a night they have had no sleep
But not a word from them, not even a peep

Get out your flowers and a meal too
Treat them as well as you know you should do
When they are gone it is for ever
So make the most of it while you're together.

Jack Sismey

UNTITLED

My mummy she is thirty
But me, I am just three
She is a very good mum
And she looks after me
She takes me to parties
And down to the park
She keeps me from bad things
And dogs that go bark
She buys me nice clothes
And good things to eat
She buys me nice toys
And shoes for my feet
She takes me to nursery
And over to gran's
We take her nice flowers
And strawberry flans
Then we go home
To make Dad his tea
He's always got kisses
For mummy and me
And then it's to bed
Because it's a dark night
My mum puts me in
And tucks me up tight
And I say my prayers
To the Lord up above
To look after Mummy
Who I so much love.

Thomas McCormick

MOTHER

A mother's love is fair and true.
She giveth of herself to you.
She's always there without a doubt,
You never have to scream or shout.
An ear to hear, a hand to hold.
Yes, even when you're growing old.
A mother's love is fair and true.
I am so glad that I have you.

G Harley

A MOTHER'S WORK

I bear, I bathe, and love in so many ways,
As well as shop and cook and clean,
Share all their worries, also their joys,[
And I'm always there to be seen.

They take me for granted, anything they want,
For all their special needs,
To clothe for school and holidays,
And applaud their special deeds!

I take them out, and entertain,
Supply the cash as well,
And when not wanted, because of friends,
I sit at home, and make and mend.

On their birthdays, I prepare the party,
Also the food and drink,
And when it's done I clean it up, over by the sink,
They take it all without even a blink!

At Christmas time, I shop till I drop,
To give a good time to all,
Feeling at times like Cinderella,
Waiting to go to the ball!

But Mother's Day is a different day,
It's my turn for the day to enjoy,
They wait on me, the whole day through,
Anything I want, from my girls and boy.

The day is wonderful, and full of joy,
To see the way, they appreciate me!
To reward me for all my work, and love,
Each Mothering Sunday, each year, for me!

The End

B W Crossman

MY LOVING MOTHER
(Dedicated to Violet Gray who died of TB 2/8/70)

I wanted to take a moment to express my love for you
for a dearest darling mother who's love is so very true
Your love has been unconditional and so very strong
and you have never rejected me even when I was wrong
Your love and affection I have never been without
and the place I hold in your heart I never had to doubt
from being a helpless little baby on your care I did depend
to this present day your support you will always lend
Through every stage in my life you always have been there
you have showed how much you love me and truly care
I was taught by you the important values of this life
and it has held me steadfast through trouble and strife
I am now independent and confident thanks to your love
the gratitude I feel for you I could never say enough
It was difficult when I grew up and time to say goodbye
I was going to make my own life we both tried not to cry
We both miss each other although we're not too far away
and I come and see you often almost every other day
Mother you are getting older now rely upon me please
it's time for you to take your life a little more at ease
now it's my chance to care for you with love and affection
as our lives start taking on this new and different direction
but all my childhood memories of you are in my heart
and so with my love so deep we will never be apart

Marlene Mullen

UNTITLED

I want to play the game of life
and be a busy, better wife
It's hard to know when to be me
I'm busy helping others, you see

I try to cook and clean and sew
But sometimes I never know
If it's good enough to be
The mainstay of our family

A person in my very own right
Has always been a mental fight
To bury myself in life's toils
Or hold out hard and collect the spoils

A happy life I've always had
When being wife and mum's not bad
But can I ever just be *me?*
And not an extension of my family!

Christina Hayes

GROWING UP

I love my Mother dearly
she's handled my 'growing up days' so well,
all the mood swings and tantrums
she must have gone through hell.
How she's coped
I will never know,
but I suppose she went through the same
just a few years ago.
I don't know what I'd do without her
she's a big part of me,
I'd do anything for her
she's what I want to be.
When I've had a hard day at school
and everything's in a muddle,
there's nothing better to come home
and have a great big cuddle.

L Starling

PLEASURES!

'Leave that alone!' 'I want a carry!'
Motherhood pleasures abound,
From cleaning up messes
To tending a sick one,
What sort of life had I found?

The horrors continued as older he got,
Next door's broken window but one,
And Grandpa to calm down
When in bed he discovered
What my little precious had done.

Now we've been to his wedding,
The bridegroom behaving his best,
But I'm sorry for me,
I miss him you see,
And the dear life I had with my pest.

Elizabeth Marriott

WE DID NOT WANT

We did not want to lose you,
although you'd had your years,
We knew we had to say goodbye
and try to hide our tears,
God knew that you were weary,
you'd often told him so,
He gently took you by the hand,
and said 'It's time to go,'
So now we have our memories
of laughter, love and fun,
so proud and happy that you reached
the age of ninety-one,
Of all the names I know and love
can't think of any other,
Than the one from God above,
and that name is my Mother.

Marjorie Britton

MUMMY

Mummy - the most beautiful word I know!
Her life in the family - always all go . . .
She cares for us morning, noon and night,
Her facial expression smiling and bright,
If something's wrong, she puts it right.

She cooks our meals and darns our socks;
If it's raining one day, there's the magic box:
Always something to do if we can't go outside,
She knows what we like and is our best guide
In this wonderful world, where pleasures abide.

My mummy's not with me here any more,
But what wonderful memories I have in store:
I know she's with God as my Guardian Angel,
Each day I am happy, in all things I revel;
Her example stays with me - I know no Hell . . .

J M Grigor

TO MUM . . . ON MY 40TH BIRTHDAY

It's forty years
Since I was born on that October day;
Through joys and tears
You've guided me and shown a loving way.
You've taken care
Of me and listened when I needed you,
Forever there
If I should want advice, to talk things through.
You gave to me
A happy home, the finest start I know,
I'll always be
So grateful for the love and trust you show.
I hope I may
Bring up my children, both in deed and thought,
In just the way
I learned at home the values which you taught.
In times of strife
You've always been the first to lend a hand;
Throughout my life
You've been the one to soothe and understand.
As life again
Begins for me today, in years to come
You will remain
Unequalled, so God bless . . . and thank you, Mum.

Wendy Hutton

MY MOTHER

My Mother, who bears the same name,
My Mother, she adds lustre, to the same
My Mother, who shares my joy
My Mother, she cheers me when I'm sad
My Mother is the greatest friend I ever had
My Mother I wish long life to her
For there's no other
Can take the place of
My Mother.

Val Taylor

UMBILICAL CORD

The umbilical cord was never cut,
I still feel you're a part of me.
All angry words spoken in haste,
Only rebound to stab my heart.

From toddler to teenager I saw you through,
and you're surprised how much I've learnt,
how modern I've become,
Remembering my Mother's words reminds me,
I thought the same.

Now together we face the world today,
Even grown-ups need to cry.
The centre of my universe,
I moved my world to be there for you.

Between cotton wool wrapped and freedom to grow,
It's a narrow line I've tried to draw.
Slowly, changes move child to teacher,
Now I learn from my prodigy.
The umbilical cord was never cut.

Carole Webster

To Mam On Mother's Day

It's Mother's day but you're not here
I think a lot and shed a tear
For times gone by both happy and sad
I remember your pain and I should be glad

I'm happy that you hurt no more
But thought for myself still comes to the fore
I miss you so much every day, every night
Will darkness pass over and let me have light

The day you slipped away from me
I was blinded by tears, I could not see
I was numb and confused part of me had just died
As I sat in despair, you sat down by my side

As you sat down beside me, I felt all your love
It came straight from God in his Heaven above
Some comfort it gave me to know you were there
A lessening of pain that I thought I could bear

Then I sensed in that room on that sorrowful day
You'd brought someone with you, to show me the way
You told me you loved me, and said 'Don't be sad'
You looked back and smiled 'I'll be alright with Dad'

It gave me such peace, eased the ache in my heart
To know that forever you would never part
I don't know where Heaven is, how near, how far
But I know for your goodness that's where you both are.

Anne Craig

UNTITLED

A precious little package
that started out as love.
A special little baby
sent from God above.
I came into this world
not knowing what to do
but everything I know now
I've learned because of you.
If I was ever hurting
If I was feeling blue
Your special Mother's touch
would always guide me through.
As we learn together
about all there is to know
this special love between us
will forever grow.
If I could choose a Mother
I'm please to say it's true
I'd never find another Mum
as wonderful as you.

Michelle Simpson

MOTHER AND CHILD

Mother, you carried me
With love for your unborn
I heard your heart beating
Your voice, soft and warm.

Mother, you delivered me,
In labour, you did not complain
You held me in your arms
Our bonding eased your pain.

Mother, you were with me
When I gave my first smile
I saw your eyes water
It nearly made you cry.

Mother, you watched me
As I stood and tried to walk
And you were so very proud
When I began to talk.

Mother, you nurtured me,
Through all my youthful years
Happiness and sadness
Sometimes pain and tears.

Mother, you always stood by me
And listened to my woes
Showed me understanding
Whichever way I chose!

Mother, you are wonderful
A precious part of me
And even when we're apart
You're where I long to be.

Mother, now I'm a mother
And I know just how you feel
There's no love like a mother's
It's an everlasting seal.

I love you Mother.

R Costello

THOUGHTS OF YOU

In your eyes I see the love
You've given to us all
In your arms I feel secure
Just like when I was small
In your smile I see the pride
You have in all I do
I thank you Mum for everything
I owe so much to you.

Susan Moore

ESSENTIAL OILS

'Mummy's flowers' are collected every day,
Pink and peach petals from a rosebud
Her hands offering concentrated love.

Sarah Ledger

WHAT'S IN A MOTHER?

What's in a 'Mother'? Let us seek,
And discover the key to the ultimate role
Which no-one can learn, but only peek
Into the 'I' of the birth-giving soul.

You learn from your Mother, it is said,
The same mistakes though intentions sincere;
There's no easy path, just follow the head,
Experience leads but is followed by fear

Of imperfect standard, not merely flawed;
To cherish and nurture are parts of the plan;
Sacrifice made, the birth pain endured,
Maternal love's cycle since time first began.

If being a Mother is unpractised Art,
then lead the way forward, you be the guide,
With nothing but instinct to follow the heart,
Can love set the pace with guilt set astride?

But what's in a 'Mother'? answer me now,
This ultimate role, where is the key?
A reason for loving, for making that vow,
The key is the child, the answer for me.

Trudy A Williams

UNTITLED

Darling Mother, I love you so
The warmth of you, the inner glow
Your goodness and your loving care
Coping always, being there
Using computers, PCs and E Mail
So strong and so clever, but looking so frail
Take care little Mother, wherever you go
And come home safely - we need you so.

Jan Beecher

MY MUM

When first I came in
to this world big and loud.
My mum held me close
and said, you make me proud.

All through my childhood
she was there with a smile.
Building me up
to face life with such style.

Encouraging me on
in the ways that are true,
And always a cuddle
when ere I was blue.

When teen years arrived
and problems did sprout
She gave me good guidance
of what life's about.

Then came the day
to give of my vows.
She stood there behind me
and welcomed my spouse.

She's still there to support me
through thick and through thin.
And always she's smiling
a big mighty grin.

So this day I salute you
a mum of the best.
And beg of you dearly
please, take a rest.

M H W Wildman

MOTHER DEAREST

When I think of you,
I feel so proud you've suffered greatly,
As seven years ago you were told,
The cancer in your bones,
You never cry but when alone,
You cover pain with a smile,
You'd even walk a mile,
You're always there to lean on,
A shoulder also to cry on,
You're not just a friend but also a very dear mother.

Sandra Pickering

ODE TO MUM

For all the unconditional things you do
And loving words you say,
This poem is for you Mum
On this special Mother's Day.

Every day should be a thank you
For all your help, support and care -
The silent tears and laughter too,
Throughout the years we always share.

You share my joy when things go well
Pride in abundance beaming from your face
You're always the first one that I tell
As I know I'll get a hearty embrace!

You pick me up when I fall down
Say the right things when I feel low
But night and day there's never a frown,
Just that special love you always show.

So for all the things I take for granted
And everything I forget to do,
I just want to say I'm glad you're my Mum
And that I love you too!

Helen Rickard

UNTITLED

Fifty million harassed mums
Watching on TV
Smiling mum with 'Fairy' hands -
Doesn't look like me!

Fifty million envious mums -
Her furniture! Her flowers!
Pretty, picture-postcard home -
Doesn't look like ours!

Fifty million happy mums
Sit and have a brew
No-one there to criticise -
Perhaps she envies you!

Irene Roberts

MOTHER'S DAY MESSAGE

Thank you for having me,
Thank you for carrying me for nine months,
Thank you for waking up in the middle of the night, when I cried.

Thank you for feeding me,
Thank you for giving me love,
Thank you for being there when times were tough,
Thank you for being my only friend.

Thank you for the laughs,
I'm not just thanking you,
Because it's Mother's Day
I'm thanking you every day of my life,
Thank you Mummy.

Love Kulsum.

Kulsum Shaikh (15)

A MOTHER'S LOVE

It started out one winter's night when he came home from school
A quiet and sombre little lad, which went against the rule.
I asked him gently what was wrong or if he felt unwell,
Call it mother's intuition, he was poorly, I could tell.

I held my arms wide open and he ran to my embrace.
He needed to be comforted, I sensed it in his face.
His little velvet cheeks were flushed, like petals of a rose,
Stroking back his golden hair, I kissed him on the nose.

'Make me better, Mummy, I don't feel well tonight.'
I hugged him close and whispered that it soon would be alright.
His skin was burning to the touch, I held his clammy hand,
Although a simple common cold, he didn't understand.

I sensed a long night faced me as I carried him to bed,
Dosed with children's medicine to ease his hurting head.
Overcome with helplessness, I gave a troubled sigh
And showered him with kisses as he then began to cry.

I knew it wasn't serious, but was painfully aware
That he might develop symptoms that at present were not there.
I snuggled down beside him, then got right in his bed
And stroked his face so tenderly, 'I love you, Mum' he said.

I told him that I loved him too, I felt my heart would burst
With thoughts of Meningitis, I dared not fear the worst.
I checked his neck and then his skin each time he gave a whine
Was it my imagination or had I seen a sign?

But finally the fever cooled, he drifted off to sleep
And drained of all emotion, I allowed myself a weep.
The worry, love and heartache are all part of the deal
And every loving mother knows, exactly how I feel.

Karen Tyas

ON MOTHER'S DAY

Dear mother of mine
You're always there for me
So Mother's Day is a big day
To show you how much I love you
(With a big bouquet)
With hugs and kisses
All through the day
I even buy you chocolates
To say to you are sweet,
And in every way
My dear mother of mine
On Mother's Day.

C C Warner

MOTHERS

A mother's love is special
So love her while you may
For I would give the world
If mine were here today.

She is there when you need her
To guide you on your way
And listen to your troubles
That might come your way.

Mother's Day is special
I know this is true
But it's not just Mother's Day
She is there for you.

So don't take her for granted
Like some people do
For you never know the day
She won't be there for you.

Elizabeth Gorman

My Mum

I recall a flowery dress
And one who cleared up all the mess
When friends came round for a jelly party
You were always there so hail and hearty

You bought me clothes that would always suit
And used to make me look quite cute
Buckets and spades down at the seaside
And a stripy outfit I wore with pride

And you'd be there when I cut my knee
You'd clean it up and comfort me
Always there to help me out
Of this I would have no doubt

And as I grew through childhood years
You gave advice to calm my fears
Not to mention yummy food
That filled a happy healthy brood

These memories will forever wind
Throughout the space that is my mind
This thank you poem is from your son
Thanks for being a smashing Mum.

Chris Hughes

ALZHEIMER'S

Are you in there, Mum?
Or have you already gone?
I hold your gaze
(You won't let me hold your hand)
Seeking some spark of recognition
In the depths of your one good eye -
So surprisingly, beautifully brown -
Trying to see if you're at home.

When you surprise us
With some well-remembered phrase
Or vehement objection,
Is it you, trying to communicate,
Or is it some old, worn-out tape
You left running when you went?

Went where?
Do you look down on your own shell
And us who loved you sitting round?
Or have you gone completely?
Worst of all, are you still trapped
Inside that useless, wasted hulk
That will not die;
Unable to tell us you are there?

Chris Gutteridge

UNTITLED

From the beginning of my time
You've always been there, always be mine.
You advise me with words that are honest and true,
And in these times and days, of those there are few.

To love, to understand, to cherish, to care,
To give a love that's unconditional and fair
From the laughter to the tears
From the smile to the fears
With a strength I would be lost without
You're there without a doubt.

And when I'm sad and blue
You help me with those troubles too,
When all I want, is to hide my face and cry
You help me keep my head held high.

And when the darkness of loneliness is real
You're the light I always feel.

All the words in the world can't express
The love and the tenderness.
The way you make me feel
When everything else is completely unreal.

What can I give back to you
Apart from these words that are simple and true.
            Mum, I love you. xx

J M Dacosta

BONJOUR MAMAN

Bonjour Maman, comment ça va
It's me, your daughter Anne
I'd like to say a big 'Merci'
You made me what I am

Bonjour Maman, comment ça va
I've sent roses and a card
I can't be there - too many miles
But you're in my thoughts and heart

Bonjour Maman, comment ça va
Now I'm a mother too
I know it is a lifetime's work
Will I succeed like you?

Bonjour Maman, comment ça va
Words don't properly bestow
My thanks for all those years of love
But thanks - a bientôt.

Anne Polhill Walton

MOTHER'S DAY
(In memory of Mrs K Bryszkiewski)

Mother dear, mother dear,
Now you are no longer here
Where can I send my thoughts to you this
Mothering Sunday?
You are with our Lord,
Smiling with the angels high.
I'm down here all alone.
Silently, sad tears I cry.
I spare a thought for daughters and sons
For those, like me, who have lost their mums.
This is a special day for me
When all I want to say is , I Love You.
By your side I cannot be
So please, Lord, say hello from me
The tears of sadness have all but gone
I'm left now with thought so sweet
Of the time when once again we meet
I know that time is far away but
The things you taught me will forever stay
It's with this line I will close
Thank you for being my mum.
     God Bless.

Franciszek Bryszkiewski

A TRIBUTE TO MOTHERS

To lose a mother is to lose, a best friend
No matter what occurs, through life
You have little quarrels, then it's time to make up
Before the sun sets, each night

Whatever she is, whether rich, or poor
Don't shun her, it's her love, that matters
Don't hold back, your feelings
Till all you hold dear, is shattered

Please listen, all you daughters
Just say a prayer, to God, above
Thank Him, for the mother, you were given
Don't ever lose, her precious love.

Vera Ewers

THE EYES OF MOTHERHOOD

Your new-born child peers at you
through innocent unseeing eyes

Your toddler's eyes wide open
with joy, frustration and surprise

Your school age child's eyes
questioning, striving to understand

Your adolescent's eyes so challenging
with anger close at hand

But the grown up child's eyes mirror
what yours did long ago

The seeds you planted way back then
you always prayed would grow

May Perkins

Our Mum's Day

It's an annual event, your own special day
Celebrating your efforts as our Mum in your way
Remembering the times in our earlier lives
When you put us before you, selfless, with pride

Always there when we needed your time and advice
You helped us untangle our problems in life
Always there to inspire us, to guide us through time
Even when you were busy you just didn't mind

All those Christmas and birthdays we had in our youth
No shortage of presents presented with love
All those outings to seasides or visits to shops
Buying the fashions seen on 'Top of the Pops'

The years have passed by we have homes of our own
Those children you mothered are all older and grown
But we still come to see you if we think you can help
Your answers much wiser, more precious than wealth

So enjoying Mothering Sunday, remember we care
We thank you for life and the times that we share
We wish you the best in the time still to come
We'll always remember our own special Mum.

Jean Ray

MORE THAN A WOMAN

More than a woman,
More than a wife,
To give a child the gift of life
Is the greatest challenge you'll ever know
All your emotions overflow
Feelings of love, relief and pure joy
But is it a girl or is it a boy?

Sue Elderton

JUST FOR MUM

Mothers are all wonderful
All children will agree.
We all love our Mothers
All through time you'll see.
When love is really needed
Your Mum is there for you.
You know that she's your best friend
Though you don't have a clue

Tell your Mum your secrets
These things for you she'll keep
She'll see you through your ups and downs
Then have a good night's sleep.
All these words I've written
Have come straight from my heart
If not for you, I'd not have been
Yours right from the start.

Elaine Marie Wilson

MUM

You gave me life my heart and soul
and years fulfilled with joy,
You gave me all a son could wish
from when I was a boy.

To me dear Mum you were unique
for words could not explain
the love I've always had for you
through sun, the wind, and rain.

I never thought you'd ever die
well surely not so soon.
I'd never felt so helpless Mum
the night the Lord took you.

Time has passed and still I cry
I am still filled with rage.
People say time heals all wounds
and life will turn a page.

I doubt it Mum, in fact I know
'cause all my love still burns.
I've really tried to be so strong
but for you this boy still yearns.

Carl Morris

My Mum

My mum is not just a parent
She is a special friend you see!
'Cause she's one I can talk to
Thirty-five years she's looked after me.

I am a mum of three now
And hope to follow her ways
Caring, helping, feeding everyone
It's hard work, but it pays.

When it comes to Mothering Sunday
I buy her something new
It's not just another present
It's to say a big thank you.

Without her there to look after us
I don't know who we would turn to
'Cause when the kids are poorly or sick
It's their gran they want not really you.

When I grow old and become a gran
And my mum's not there to talk with
I hope I can follow her footsteps
To care and love as long as I live.

H Yates

MOTHER AND ME

I looked down in awe as you held me in your hand,
Looking up with wonder at this tiny child, God made,
And gave you to own till old enough to own itself.

Down the years to come you never understood,
You wanted me so perfect,
But I never could.

Now with home of my own,
And children full grown,
I look back at mistakes I've made.

Rebellious years over, at last I understand,
How hard it was to hold my hand,
And wait for me, to find myself.

P Merrill

AS REGARDS A MOTHER

A mother is a timeless machine
With hands that guide, cook, work, keep clean
The children placed into her care, and in whose daily life does share
Her love, her aims, her hopes, that they will care, and for the future
To come, generation of children, also given them

A mother is a friend indeed
Who in supplying all our need
Goes on to care, even when her breed
Are independent, self-sufficient, parents themselves then becoming
A debt is owed, that cannot be paid, as they only ask that in us is
displayed
That same loving and caring, that has in fact made, what I would call
A *Real Mother* and *Father.*

M Lightbody

MOTHER'S MEMORIES

Memories of my mother
I do recall,
Watchful eyes for us all,
Hard times, starting out,
Could mean death or life,
Keep straight and tall
Like the flowers in the garden
I do recall,
Beautiful blooms,
Fragrant times,
Sad they were left behind.
Like the snowdrops
She still lives on
A white stone in her memory
My mother's never gone!

She still lives on!

Lynda Marjoret Firth

HANDS - DEVOTION

The hands that first
cradled me after birth
with that assuring touch
warm and tender,
making me feel safe and secure.
The hands that led me
to my first day at school,
the hardest thing of all to do
was let go of those precious hands,
with sadness and joy,
I walked into the big wide world,
Those hands are of my loving mother
that give unconditional love,
something invaluable and priceless.

Aysha Rubeena Suraiyya (12)

UNTITLED

Mum he's hitting me again,
now he's just pulled my hair.
The baby's got your make-up bag,
there's lipstick on the chair.
I'm hungry when will dinner be?
Oh you know I don't like peas.
I need a drink of water,
Can I have a biscuit please?
Have you got my shirt clean yet,
from the bolognaise sauce?
What do you mean where is it!
On my bedroom floor of course.
Why can't she go round the shops?
Why is it always me?
Don't worry Mum I'll go for you,
you have a cup of tea.
It's Sunday Mum here's a cuppa
have a nice lie in.
I've made myself some breakfast
Can I get you anything?
Give me a great big cuddle Mum,
I love you loads I do.
When I grow up and I'm a man
I'm gonna marry you.

Julie Mowatt

BE STILL CHILD

Be still child, still and calm
for I am your mother and I am here
to soothe away the fear of night dreams
spun and woven from your father's bitter seed.

Be still child, for as my son
I hold you close in the warmth of my blood and soul.
You are my spirit. You are my flesh
and shall become my grail and constant cause
from that first sweet second when your cry of life
is born with thankful prayers
and delivered to the Mother goddess of the Moon.

Be still, my child . . . I feel your impatience to begin
but the stars must turn
through one last cycle to come full term
before I lose you to the world.

Be still, be gentle.
For me, this time is the only time
when though not yet born but still so vital and alive
you are one with me and truly mine,
mine alone to cherish.

J Christie

MOTHER'S DAY WISH

It's Mother's Day once more,
It's the day we remember who brought us into the world.
With their smiling faces of joy - we see,
And who takes care of you and me.
Remembering how she bounced us on her knee,
This day we remember them.
With our cards and flowers
And tell them you love them still,
After all these years.
And give them a special Mother's day lunch,
Treat them like Queens
So let's not forget them each and every one
And say Happy Mother's Day.

Ann Best

MY MUM

Mum can laugh and she can cry
She'll give her love until she dies
She's my mum

Mum can bake and cook steak
Fill me till my body aches
She's my mum

Mum makes gravy that's just right
Her puddings like dynamite
Oh what a wonderful sight
She's my mum

Mum can wash and she can sew
Makes my heart all aglow
She loves me of this I know
She's my mum

Mum is married to my dad
I bet he's really glad
Always happy never sad
She's my mum

Without her I wouldn't be
She shines so I can see
Shields herself in front of me
That's because she's my mum.

Numero Uno

SUMMER

Summer is the time when Mother Earth makes ready to
give of her rosy fruits and golden grain.
Summer is a time of warm, lazy days by the sparkling sea,
restful days by a cool, deep lake.
I opened my arms to the warmth of God's love,
and found perfect rest, on such a day as one of these.
So, when you think of me, think of summer.
When the breeze rustles the leaves, and stirs your hair,
I will be there, touching you.
I will still join the birds in their sweet praise for
the gift of another new day.
As you look into the heart of a flower you will find me,
gazing up into your eyes.
Remember those crystal dewdrops are but tears
for my new found joy.
Every golden sunset is but the reflection of newly found peace.
Each quiet, rosy dawn renews my promise to you of a new,
everlasting life.
Do not sigh, for I have left behind my fruit,
My grain - my harvest to your world -
I leave with you a mother's love and by doing this .
How will I ever leave you?

Margaret Poole

ALMOST TOO GOOD TO BE TRUE

She's always there when I need a hug,
And her point of view.
She always gives me a helping hand.
She's almost too good to be true.

She mops my brow when I'm ill,
And feeds me when I'm there.
I shouldn't take for granted though,
Her loving and her care.

She helps me out in times of strife,
And helps keep me on my feet.
It's no wonder really,
That everyone thinks she's neat.

Vicky Wood

THREE CHEERS FOR OUR MUM

When all of us were younger Mum
You always worked so hard,
Not only taking care of us
But holding down a job.
Our dad was self-employed back then
Which meant sometimes his wage
Was lower than the week before
Which made you feel afraid.
You knew if you kept working though
As well as helping Dad,
You could also pay for all of us
To go on trips as well.
But when you went out shopping Mum
You always thought of us
Returning home with sweets and comics
And some food of course.
But now that we're all older
We feel so sad to see
Because you helped us all so much
You couldn't save a thing.
We hope one day you'll get to know
Exactly how it feels
To spend some money on yourself
Instead of all your bills.
It's time you had some pleasure too
Before you pass away
As no mum's more deserving
Than you are every day.

Merilyn Gulley

EARTH MOTHER

The person of which I am about to speak,
Is special to me and is truly believed,
Her grace lovingly coverts her aura,
And has many a time been seen,
For this person is my mother,
Whom I sincerely love so deep.
Constantly attached to this woman,
Having respect for what she's endured,
With comforting eyes, and words so soft,
All my anguishes she has cured.
Very proud to be moulded in her image,
As she's made my life complete,
Being a part of my mother so dear,
Never will my love for her retreat.

My 'Mother's Day' message is lovingly meant,
And from deep in my heart to you it is sent.
So proud of the fact that you are my mum,
Enjoy the day thoroughly, as you're number one.

Louise Brown

MOTHER MINE

My mother was good to us all,
She helped us when we had a fall,
Taught us all to be good and kind,
And had it always in her mind
To teach us to do right, be good,
To obey her, we knew we should
Showed us how to help each other,
We thank God for our loving mother.
She cooked well, we had such good food,
We quarrelled, were not always good,
But she showed us how to forgive,
Then in loving kindness to live.
She taught us how to help others,
She was the best of all mothers!

Lilian M Loftus

MOTHER

(Dedicated to my mother, Ruth Bennet who passed away.
Gone but never forgotten)

You gave me life,
And through the years . . .
You saw me through,
My hopes and fears.

You gave me love,
And eased my pain.
Your love for me,
It never waned.

You gave me courage,
To see things through.
All my strength,
I learnt from you.

You gave me hope,
When all looked dark.
You tenderly nursed
My broken hearts.

Then one cold November day,
The *angels* came and took you away.
My life, my love, my hope all gone,
But my courage remained . . . to carry on.

You gave me many gifts in life,
That I can share in being *mother* and *wife*.
You gave me the gift of loving sisters and brothers,
I am so proud . . . to call you mother.

Tracy Bell

A DIAMOND OR A PEARL?

There are people in this world who like diamonds,
There are people in this world who like pearls.
There was someone who liked anything, that sparkled, just the same,
Like the eyes of that sweet old fashioned girl.

No matter what the time or day,
You would never hear her say,
The lonely word of 'No' or 'Sorry I must go.'
In that old sofa chair,
You'd always find her sitting there.

'I guess there'll always be a little bit missing,
Now that Mum has finally gone away,
But I'm not sitting around and keep on wishing,
For I know she wouldn't want it, not that way.'

I am grateful for the love that's now gone missing,
It will be the finest jewel in my heart,
You could never buy this feeling that I'm missing,
It will stay with me, and fill that missing part.

There are people in this world who love diamonds,
There are people in this world who love pearls,
But I will always love the eyes that sparkled, just the same,
From the smile of that sweet old fashioned girl.

I ask you my friend to say, which would you choose today,
A diamond or a pearl, or a sweet old fashioned girl?
With a love so rare, you always knew would be there,
From the sweetest little lady in the world.

Jessie Morton

THREE CHEERS FOR MUM

Let us hear it loud and clear,
Remembering, who dried our every tear.

Cuts, bruises, broken hearts, a salve for every pain,
Her love sheltering us from life's inevitable rain.

A glance in the direction of the stick,
Between naughty or obedient guided our pick.

The threat to use it was enough, for you to choose,
Your mum's love is such, the stick would her also, bruise.

That stopped you from being bad,
Because, you don't like to see mum sad.

That's the reason you don't make scenes,
When Mum tells you to eat up your greens.

The same when ordered to your teeth brush,
Bite your tongue to any complaints hush.

When told to go and put on your vest,
You do not call your mum a pest.

Grown up, you will look back with adult sight,
And see your mum, in her wisdom, was always right!

Joy R Gunstone

MOTHER

As an only child
I had an infinite need of others,
to be allowed in, surrounded and loved.
And I was grateful when
in later years,
you accorded me the dignity of trust,
by silencing your own fears.

And through your eyes
I saw the touch of genius,
a seed already sown.
Always aware of my ambitions,
you were preoccupied
with any glory
but that of your own.

With the passing of time,
I have distanced myself little
by little from you, and from
the image to which I belong.
But the former is still engraved
in my heart in tender letters,
to cradle me like a song.

Anne Palmer

MOTHER

M is for Mum, the best in the world,
O is for ours, to love and to hold.
T is for treasure, because that's what you are,
H is for honest, so honest by far.
E is for eternal, the love I have for you,
R is for respect, today and my life through.

Christine Sinclair

LADY OF THE FLOWERS

How you loved your flowers, Mum,
Your garden was so bright.
You tended it with loving care,
And always got it right.
Pruning, weeding, watering,
Smelling a favourite rose.
We would always find you working,
How you managed it no-one knows.
I've bought some flowers for Mother's Day,
The way I always do.
They look so bright and cheerful,
Reminding me, Mother, of you.
Your life was not so easy,
You had your cross to bear.
When things became too hard to take
God called you into his care.
With tear-filled eyes I remember,
Your face, weary, but smiling and brave.
My love will reach you in Heaven,
As pretty flowers I place on your grave.

Joy Cooke

MY MOTHER'S LOVE

From a babe in arms to womanhood
My mother always understood
Her shining love is always there
From the day I was born she loved and cared
The love that came from my mother's heart
Was there right from the very start
She was always loving, caring and giving
To help with my life amongst the living
If I could only turn back the clock to when I was small
And dwell on the memories I now re-call
Mother of mine be here by my side
Always and ever to comfort and guide
I miss the love you gave to me
Your wonderful smile as I sat on your knee
I don't know why you had to go
Only God will ever know
Goodnight sweet dreams dear mother of mine
My love for you will always shine.

Jean Carswell

MOTHERS

Mothers are such a precious thing,
We learn as we grow older.
They always lend a helping hand,
And a comforting shoulder.

They cook and clean and sew for us,
And nurse us when we are ill
Put a bandage on a damaged knee,
For headaches give us a pill.

They watch us as we grow from
Childhood to teens,
And try to understand
Just how we feel when growing up,
Waiting with guiding hand.

It's only when we are mothers
                           ourselves,
That we fully understand
Just what being a mother means,
With younger lives in our hands.

Iris Covell

RESPITE CARE

We chat away of this and that,
your ailments and the weather.
I've brought you your old shady hat
and a potted lilac heather.

We admire the roses' lovely scent
that grow beneath your window,
when, conversation almost spent,
and I'm getting up to go,

You look at me with my grey eyes
and ask 'Tell me, how's your mother?'
'She's you,' I say to your surprise,
'And I'd never want another.'

For 'though you don't know me, still,
one day soon, too soon, you will.

Lesley James

MUM'S THE WORD

My mum has been an inspiration to me,
She taught me things that need to be,
In things I've done right and wrong,
the worry and stress I did prolong.
In my teens I wanted things my way,
and didn't listen to what she'd say,
and so we drifted separately apart,
breaking both our own emotional heart.
At present we no longer moan,
and our love has strongly grown,
In fact we're both quite the same,
and for that I'm sure not to blame.
We now hide no barrier to screen,
We're closer than ever has been,
We now seem to correspond,
Mother and child, that's the bond.

Nichole Jackman

A Tribute To My Mother

Friend, companion and teacher.
Trust and care.
There is no other
Like my dear mother.
To have one's heart
in the right place.
Enter into the feelings of others.
Treat well.
The best intentions.
You brought me up
with loving kindness.
Blessings to our Saviour
On this our day of rest.
Sunday school three times a day
when I was young
and led the right way.
The message from God
Pouring love from above.
Holy Dove.
For my dear Mother.

Pat Jones

DEVOTION

Mothers are full of mixed emotions,
But whose love one cannot compare,
For wherever you go or what you do,
You will always take her love there!

Sometimes we may make her laugh,
Then other times we make her cry.
But the bond is so secure that,
You know her love will never die!

Someone to share all your troubles,
Plus tease and torment and have fun.
But life would be lonely and empty,
Without your special treasured mum!

None of us appreciate what we have,
Just expect her to always be there
Because mothers are special people
So show respect to prove you care!

Ann Beard

IN MEMORY OF HER

Once in the evening glow
Her radiant face
Caressed me with a slow
And gentle grace.

And once in winter's gloom
Her smiling eyes
Burnished the cheerless room
Where memory lies.

Now in the dust of years,
With barren hearts,
My vision blurs with tears
As joy departs.

And April flowers wear
A sombre hue;
If joy is buried there,
My life is, too.

Yet in a fairer day
Her soul will ride
The vast, eternal way,
With bliss as guide.

O jewel in my crown,
This heart beguile,
Lest love and laughter drown
Without your smile.

S H Smith

A TIRED LITTLE LADY
(Dedicated to my mum, Glynis)

What's the matter, why are you sad?
Is it a pain that's hurting so bad
Please be honest and open up to me
Is it a loneliness that I can't see
What's the matter, are you dying inside?
Is it a fear you have to hide?
Have you no money day after day?
Is it a worry you have to pay?
What's the matter, you're not the same?
Is your heart tired and weary with pain?
Have you had a hard day where you've been?
Is it another speck of dust you had to clean?
What's the matter, there's something wrong?
Is it something sad 'cos your smile has gone?
Rest your head and bring out your tears
Is every drop you cry a fear?
Think about yourself once in while
Think about your precious times and smile
But all that matters to me now is what you do
And soon you'll remember that's why I love you.

Janine Dickinson

MUM'S SEVENTY TODAY

Today you would have been seventy
I can't take you out for a meal
I can't wish you happy birthday
Or ask you how you feel.

But I'm cooking a Chinese meal
Especially for you
You'll have the best seat in the house
The balcony, with the best view.

I'm celebrating your birthday
Just the same as if you were here
It'll put a smile on my face
And make you feel ever near.

And at the end of your birthday
A day that'll be cheery and bright
I'll send you this special message
I love you, sweet dreams and goodnight.

Shirley Lidbetter

MOTHER

I would not have missed being a mother
The job is more satisfying than any other
Tiny lives solely dependent
From birth until they become independent
To be responsible knowing you could make or mar
By the way you act, by the way you are
When the offspring grows up and leaves the nest
They will know who they love the best
There surely cannot be another
With unconditional love
Like their dearest mother.

Evelyn A Evans

TO THE WORLD'S BEST MUMMY

Mummy I bought you flowers
so you know and show how much
you really care for me.
You're a mummy and one in a million
I bought you roses
The red one is for love
Mummy I'm only *six,*
and you love me
You're there when I need
a helping hand
In the summer you take me
and Lisa swimming
You never leave our side
In autumn you take me to
the firework displays
You hold me if I get frightened
You cuddle me when I'm ill.
In winter Mummy you show
your love, you buy me gloves
hat and scarf to keep me warm.
I can say this today Mummy
and every year that's ahead
You're the best mummy
in this wide world
I love you Mummy
Happy Mother's Day.

Debra Wyatt (6)

YOU'RE ALWAYS NEAR US MUM

You're always close beside us
In everything we do
You were the world's
Best love Mum
God's gift to us was you.

Mum, your face was like a shining star
No matter Mum I am your little angel
Mum you were never too far away
No matter how long you might have gone
You're always there near beside me

My Mum always called me an angel
No matter if I'd done wrong
Your smiling face
Would tell it all
My Mum is one in a million.
Happy Mother's Day.

Lisa Wyatt

MY MOTHER IN REFLECTION

As I gaze into her hazel eyes
I see a reflection of myself;
Though we are a generation apart
Our values and morals are strangely,
But naturally alike, and
Like my Mother, I admit
My moods are hazardous and variable:
But on a stranger note, we both
Love and trust freely and unconditionally.
Even when we are parted
The bond that lies between us
Bridges the gap and keeps us close.
No-one loves like a mother, but
No-one can return that love
Like a mother's child.

Chrissi

MY MOTHER AND I

(My mum) Elizabeth Jane,
was her lovely name,
If ever I was naughty,
she showed she cared just the same;
She never ever smacked me
(I was her little pal),
And she always said,
she was glad I was a gal.
I did try to be good,
my brother Gordon did tease me,
She said that he would,
'Do not go near him,'
She often would say,
but I was headstrong
and liked my own way.
He told me to tell him
if someone hurt me,
He would not stand for that,
I used to wheel out in
my doll's pram our grey tabby cat,
dressed in my doll's clothes;
He'd lay asleep, I would quite often;
Just take a peep, I did not hurt Timmy,
I did really care; and pussies as dollies
                    are really quite rare.

Sheila Thompson

THANKS

Every mother is important to her child(ren) and
every child is important to their mother
There's always that special bond between them
that can never be broken.

Every family is different,
Some have better relationships than others
It may depend on what's happened in life
In my case we've become much closer.

When I was younger my papa died
then soon after my dad and
When we thought things couldn't get any worse
I became rather ill.

My Mum supported me through thick and thin
and when I was down she understood
I don't think I could have come through what I did
if she hadn't been there to support me.

Being assessed for a lung transplant
it felt like the end of the world
It was the one time I needed her most
and she was there as usual.

I'd just like to say a big 'Thank you' Mum
You really do make a difference.
I know I've got more difficult times to face
and that you'll be there to help me.

I love you Mum . . . forever.

Denise O'Donnell

A Mum Is Special

A

Mum
Understands problems
More than anyone else, she

Is
Special,

Supportive,
Puts up with moods, and
Expects nothing in return,
Caring for her children
Is a priority,
And she always give so much
Love.

Linda Casey

MOTHER

Mother Nature
Mother Earth
And Mothers of our own
All have a place in the scheme of things
The trouble is . . .
We can take them all for granted.
Do we really appreciate them?
Probably not - until it's too late
Only then do we realise
Just how much they meant to us.

It's too late when they're dead and gone
To do or say all those things we should have done.
If only we could turn those clocks back
And put to rights all those wrongs
But that's not possible.
So we have to try to live with it
Put it down to experience
And hold on to the memories.

Mother
You gave structure to my life
And showed interest in all that I tried
You've left this world now
But forgotten you're certainly not.

Mary A Slater

MOTHER

Mother's very clever she knows
All there is to know
She knows what I am thinking
But I'm sure it does not show.

She knows when I am naughty
Even when she is not there
She always seems to find out
No matter how or where.

She seems to know who pushed
Even knows when I fall
When she isn't in the room
I'm sure she can see through walls

Yet I wouldn't change a thing
Even if I could
Because Mother always knows
When I'm trying to be good.

David Sheasby

MOTHER

You give me a life, to live to the full.
At times I know, it has been far from dull.
Some things happen, maybe we do not see eye to eye.
You and me, should never say goodbye.

Now that I see things from a mother's point of view.
I clearly see, why you do some of the things you do.
In this life, I know you want me to succeed
As you're always around, when I'm in need.

In bad times, you always have an ear
With warming words, that fill me full of cheer.
You are the one, who gives me my 'get up and go'
I want you to know Mum, my love for you will
                                    never cease to grow.

A Smith

UNTITLED

A spark it takes, the growth commences
Growing by the second in size
And after hibernation
Comes the day you see their eyes
Warmth and food, love and care
Growing by the second in size
And after the first few years
They talk into your eyes.

You care, you nurture,
You control for their own good
Emotionally growing by the second in size
They leave, you care from a distant post
Then there comes a time when you
                        become less lost
They tell you about a spark,
The growth commences
And after hibernation
Comes the day you see their eyes
Warmth and food, love and care
Growing by the second in size
And all the care and nurturing
Is done by those first eyes.

The spark, the growth, the love and care
The eyes are all the same
And ever onward, the pattern goes on
And all because of *Mum.*

Maria Waters

WHY IS IT THAT MOTHERS ALWAYS UNDERSTAND

Why is it that mothers always understand,
What you are feeling when you are sad,
Why you are happy, why you are glad.

Why is it that mothers always understand,
Why your room is in such a state,
And your homework's always late.

Why is it that mothers always understand,
Why your clothes always end up on the floor,
So she can't get through your bedroom door.

Why is it that mothers always understand,
Why her favourite vase is in the bin,
She soon creates a terrible din.

Why is it that mothers always understand,
Why the new carpet's covered in dirt,
And why there's soil on your shirt.

Why is it that mothers always understand,
Why you need your own phone,
And when the bill comes, there's a groan?

Angela Bastiani

THREE CHEERS FOR MUM

We do so miss her
Everyone who knew her would agree

No matter how busy she was you knew
She always was there for you

Why am I living so long sometimes she would say
How do you know
Well it was not because she sat around
Mum was always on the 'go'.

Our mother had such a sweet voice
Sang while she did her chores
Did not scream
Knew all the words
In fact at 95
We were just glad she had her faculties
                        and was still alive

Dad gassed in First World War
His sister Caroline used to say Mum's
                        cooking kept him going
He worked hard, Sarah Georgina (Mum)
Certainly could not have done more.

Queuing, cooking, working during Second War
Seemed to come natural
We came home to wonderful meals regularly
She would never say if she was tired
Mum managed the rationing so well

Personal letters also say a great deal
My husband wrote about her
She sang, she cooked and always had a smile
And a cheerful word
So intelligent, much faith, honesty and good living
And a Giver
A Survivor!

Phyllis O'Connell

365 DAYS AND A QUARTER PLUS

Your old mum is she always there for you
365 days of the year?
In sunshine and rain in sickness and in health
Will she soothe and wipe your tears away?
You might be a child or a teenager
You might be a person in your so-called middle age
You could be in retirement yes, even over 65 years of age
Is your mum always there for you I hope she is
You never grow up you are still her child even
when you are well over 65 years of age
No matter what, in good times and bad
You will find her she might have grown old
Silver-haired in her old rocking chair she sits
You might live now hundreds of miles away
Or over the sea in far-off lands
But don't forget she's only a step away
A letter, a card, a phone call
You could make your old mum's day.
The Bible says honour your father and mother
Some people can do this with respect
But some children who have been ill-treated
By their parents in childhood
How can that child have honour or respect?

Donald Jay

MOTHER

I have a wonderful mother
Who means all the world to me
She nurses me through my illness
And invites my friends to tea.

She makes me do what I am told
And always knows the best
As I grow up I will learn
When I meet up with all the rest.

How very tired she must be
When I realise what she does
It's my turn now to repay her
For the help she's given me.

We will give her a cup of tea in bed
And wait upon her instead
Make a fuss of her this special day
She will remember come what may.

It's our Mother's day today
She deserves the very best
We are taking her on holiday
To have a well-earned rest.

Lydia McCubbin

MOTHER TO DAUGHTER
IS THERE A SPARE ROOM IN YOUR HEART?

I know your social nature
Keeps you busy.
Could you forget what's
Not worth keeping defined
And neatly blur the outline,
Of the pictures in your mind
Since few truths can be simply
Stated, and remain kind.
Above I love you, can hang
No cloud of doubt.

I try boldly to honestly express,
Though some complex questions
Never can be answered,
Led by a plain 'No!'
Or a plain 'Yes!'
If I wrote a song that
Housed itself amongst the people,
I'd be far more pleased in part,
Were it to take a room
                    within your heart.

Linda Coleman

MUM

There could never have been
any other mother for me,
What a mum, loved her so,
Me, the eldest of five,
all of us happy to be alive.
A mum, such fun,
made us all feel number one.
Girl, boy, boy, 'boy-girl' twins
at last a sister 'jealousy a little blister'
Our dear mum treated us all the same
always there for us never made a fuss
How I wish she were here today to say
'Don't worry, all will be OK.'
Never ever talked bad of anyone.
I wish all children a mum like my mum.

Valvy Hope

TO A NEW MUM

You think, of pink
And new, baby blue
Being a mum
It's a dream come true.

She'll be sweet,
He'll be cute
Be it boy
Be it girl
You're preparing the nest
In a pre-natal whirl.

Then she comes
Then he comes
Now at last you're a mother,
So ecstatic, this babe
Is unlike any other.

The years pass, life goes on
They develop and grow
And sometimes the hardest
Is just letting go.

J Facchini

MY MOTHER

I shall always remember my mother
For I was her favourite son,
My brother had died, and I'm told that she cried,
He was older - just eight - I was one.

I never remembered my brother
Nor realised all of her pain
But I was her treasure - in infinite measure
She started all over again.

She gave me her love - undivided,
More caring than ever, it seems,
As if she would strive even harder
To realise all of my dreams.

My childhood was blissfully happy
As she made a new life with my dad
Determined the shadow of sorrow
Would not touch me, or make me feel sad

And so that is how I remember
Her love, on each Mother's Day
The love she gave me in such measure
Until sadly, she passed away.

L Coleman

EVERLASTING LOVE FOR MY MOTHER

Mother was a pillar of strength
Would go to any length
To help me when in need
A real tender friend indeed.

Always when trouble was brewing
Would she give me advice so I
            knew what I was doing
Kind and divine words spoken
When my poor heart was broken.

Watchful for any evil motive
Mother always broke the ice when
                I became remotive,
'Tell me darling, what's the trouble
I will burst this troublesome bubble.'

I would answer and tell to her
                all my strife
That I had to bear
At once a bright smile would
                appear on her face
'Let the trouble stay with me
        darling, first give it some space!'

I would come home from work shattered
Mother's greeting would be
'Oh! I have gathered your pros and cons
they are not worthy of thought
                let them be bygones!'

Mother would give her last penny
To help a friend or me
Tenderness was her first thought
She would help another mother
        whose heart was thwarted.

I wish my dear Mother was still here
Her pleasant smile and sphere
Of brilliant light would brighten my day
If only she were here today!

Alma Montgomery Frank

THIS SPECIAL TIME OF YEAR

This special time of year's for you
To show how much we love you too
Gifts are sent to show you're dear
Knowing that you are always near,
The whole year through.

Cards are written from us to you
With a message so touching, don't
                                shed a tear.
Although it's not always made so clear,
This special time of year.

Flowers arrive in bunches of two
Some of yellow, some of blue.
Words are spoken, words we hear
So very special, so very dear.
A big 'Thank you' Mother, we say to you,
                        this special time of year.

Rebecca Murby

MOTHERS

Many roles of motherhood
make it a very special life,
from the moment baby's placed in our arms,
through their joys, their sorrows, their strife.

Motherhood's a mixture, see,
of happy times *and* woes,
balancing one with the other,
for that's how life goes.
Until we've learnt some sadness
we know not the value of joy;
and when we share their laughter and tears
we're still *our* Mum's girl or boy.
Nurse and teacher, sitter too,
a few of the tasks mothers share;
reading and learning together thro' life,
letting them know we care;
teaching encouragement, honesty,
patience and truth and love,
becoming a friend in their teenage years -
not easy - good heaven's above!

Many roles of motherhood
make life a special phase
that changes as our children grow
and develop *their* grown-up ways.
Whatever the relationship,
Mothers we'll *always* be,
yet in Motherhood *we're* children still, too,
Guess that's how it's meant to be!

Ann Voaden

Our Mum

Still a child who bore a child, it seems so unfair,
She never got to live her youth, before we were there,
Thrown into Motherhood, at the tender age of eighteen,
All the children she had did number up to thirteen,
She worked so hard to give us love and everything
                                                    we did need,
Without a thought for herself, indeed she knew no greed.
Now the years have gone past and her family continues to grow,
There's no call for us to ask, because we all do know,
That special love you give us, has caused us to adore,
And with each day you live, we love you even more.

Pauline Uprichard

MOTHER'S DAY

A bunch of yellow daffodils
cannot begin to say
the words I really want to find
for you on Mother's Day.

These flowers will slowly fade and die
but of one thing I'm sure.
My love for you and all you are
will last for evermore.

You set me on the path of life
before my feet could stand,
and every time I've been in need
you've gently held my hand.

You've been an extra special Mum,
for all you've had you've shared.
Though times were hard, you sacrificed
and through it all you cared.

You fed and watered me each day
and watched me as I grew.
Then when you slowly loosened strings
the time was right - You knew.

As years go by I'm learning still
how much you mean to me.
You are my help, my rock, my friend.
The best that one can be.

So yes, a bunch of daffodils
but that's a tiny part,
for most of all, on Mother's Day
is love straight from my heart.

John Christopher

MOTHERING SUNDAY

I can't bring any flowers Mum or even send a card,
I know for many who have lost their Mum this day will be hard.
We who've lost our Mothers wish they were still here,
We'd love to go and visit them and give them a word of cheer.

I remember when on Mothering Sunday and I was only small,
I'd give you a card or gift, it wasn't much at all.
You used to say 'It doesn't matter even if it only cost a penny,
It's the fact that you've remembered me, for some Mums
                                        don't get any.'

You went to be with Jesus many years ago,
Our children don't remember you, for you had to go.
Jesus called you to be with Him in His home beyond the sky,
I often wonder why He took you and left us here to cry.

I often tell our children of the things you used to do,
There've been times when it's been hard and I've really needed you.
I've told them how you taught the children how to sing
Praises to Our Father God and Jesus Our Lord and King.

The faith that you have taught me has often pulled me through,
Without my faith in Jesus, I don't know what I'd do.
So thank you Mum for all you did in teaching of God's love,
I know that some day soon I shall meet you in His home above.

Jean Parkey

INFORMATION

We hope you have enjoyed reading this book - and that you will continue to enjoy it in the coming years.

If you like reading and writing poetry drop us a line, or give us a call, and we'll send you a free information pack.

Write to :-
Anchor Books Information
1-2 Wainman Road
Woodston
Peterborough
PE2 7BU
(01733) 230761